TO THE RAILWAY BORN

TO THE RAILWAY BORN

Reminiscences of station life, 1934-92

Tony Carter

Silver Link Publishing Ltd

First published in June 1992

British Library Cataloguing in Publication Data
Carter, Tony
To the Railway Born: Reminiscences of Station Life, 1934-92
I. Title
385.0942

ISBN 0 947971 79 3

Silver Link Publishing Ltd
The Trundle
Ringstead Road
Great Addington
Kettering
Northamptonshire NN14 4BW

Printed and bound in Great Britain by
Woolnough Bookbinding Ltd,
Irthlingborough, Northamptonshire

CONTENTS

ACKNOWLEDGEMENTS

I suppose when anyone writes their first - and perhaps only - book, they surprise themselves, and are often asked 'How did you come to write it?' I had given a few talks to our local railway society and someone said 'You ought to write a book about those stories'. As some of the happenings were unique, I thought 'Why not?'

I had no idea how to go about it, and I am grateful for the help given me by John Kennedy Melling - amongst others - and, of course, Will Adams, Editor with Silver Link Publishing Ltd, for his patience and helpfulness. I would also like to express my thanks to my daughter Shelagh and her husband Andrew for the typing and 'running off', to the characters in my tales, without whom there would be no story, and to my wife Mary for putting up with my demands on her time.

Many thanks, also, to those who supplied tickets (especially Herbert Lingwood), labels, photographs and other items so promptly. I hope I have acknowledged all the illustrative material correctly - if not, I can only crave your forgiveness.

FOREWORD

by

David Jones MBE

This book is compulsory reading for all railway enthusiasts. It describes over 50 years of railway life and gives readers a professional and sometimes confidential view behind the scenes.

The title chosen for the book is admirable as it takes the reader through the constantly changing times of the former Southern Railway from pre-Nationalisation to the present day. At a time when privatisation is being seriously considered, this book could become an account of station life throughout the whole of public ownership!

Tony Carter describes his career from the lowly beginnings of a Junior Clerk to his appointments as Station Master, Instructor and Senior Clerical Officer. He recalls in great detail the many steam locomotives that he has seen and worked with, and has many amusing stories to relate, particularly during the time when the railway was a common carrier.

Railwaymen and enthusiasts alike will appreciate his description of early signalling and operating methods, and will be fascinated by the views behind the scenes at London Bridge, one of the country's busiest stations.

During my 43 years on the railway I have experienced many of the situations described in this book. It has brought back many happy memories.

David Jones started as a Junior Clerk at Sidmouth Junction (now Feniton) station and took his first station master's appointment at Seaton. When the line was closed in 1966 he transferred to Kent where he held several station master's posts. He was Area Manager at Orpington until his retirement.

1.
SEATON JUNCTION 1934-39
Childhood memories

It is difficult to know when I first became interested in railways. I have been told that I was carried up to the signal box before I was old enough to walk.

My father was station master at Seaton Junction (between Axminster and Honiton) and I was born in the station house. It was a delightful place, very much in the country, and had a large garden stretching right down to the Colyton Road. There was no bathroom (we would pump the water into the kitchen with the use of a pump outside the back door) and electricity was installed shortly before we left, just prior to the outbreak of war in 1939.

Thinking back, I suppose the light of oil lamps was scarcely sufficient to see to read or sew, but I never heard my parents complain. The dining room faced the road and the sitting room looked out over the up platform. The windows had enormous wooden shutters behind which we imagined were countless beetles and spiders, but I did not dare to find out as they were never used.

The garden had a gate to the platform (built into a concrete wall) from which we could go out at the last minute when a train ran in if we were going out for the day. We usually took a weekly shopping trip to Exeter and occasionally up to Axminster for a haircut or whatever the situation demanded. We did make the occasional trip to London when the best suit was the order of the day.

A journey to Seaton, where we had a beach hut, meant crossing the bridge, and I well remember an occasion when my mother, brother and I missed the train because it went early. We complained to my father who said 'Well, the London train was in and I knew no one from the village would be going so I let it go'!

My father, Alf Carter, station master at Seaton Junction, in the mid-1930s. Note the wide platforms and long canopies. ***Author***

The station had been rebuilt a few years earlier with two long centre passing loops and electric light. An inspector was provided in the signal box on summer Saturdays to regulate the overtaking of some of the numerous trains to and from Waterloo run-

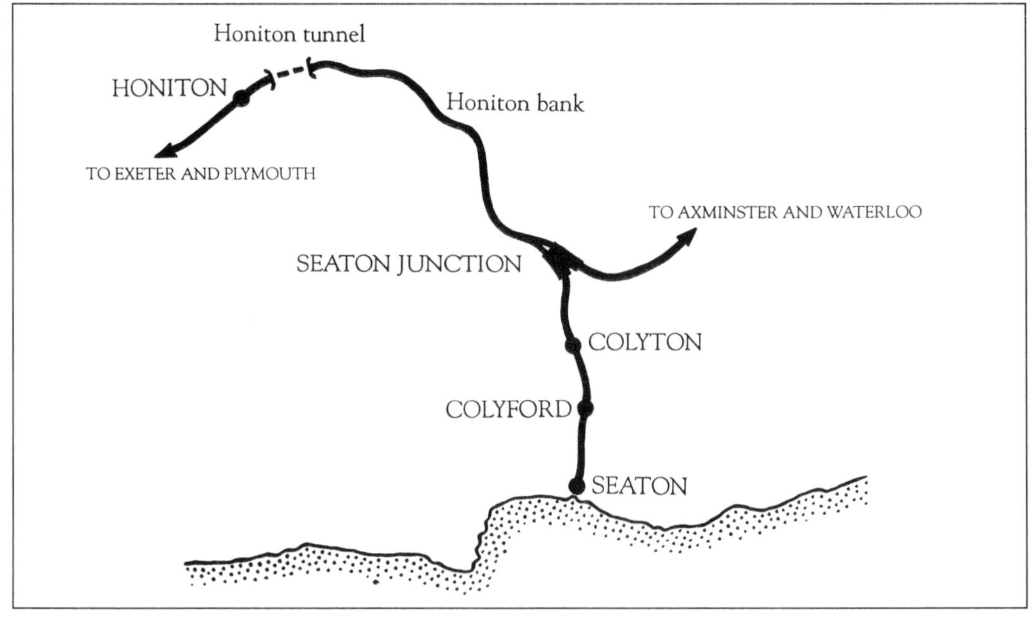

Lines around Seaton Junction. *Christina Siviter*

Seaton Junction looking east in 1938. A refreshment room was situated to the left of the signal box. Two identical footbridges can be seen, one running from the front of the station and going to the fields beyond. *Author*

Seaton Junction looking west. The station had a comparatively short life in its later form; rebuilt in the late 1920s with two through lines, it closed on 7 March 1966. *Author*

A view of Seaton Junction from the Colyton Road bridge in 1985. Note the solitary track where previously there had been four. At the time of writing plans are in hand to double the line again from Chard Junction to Seaton Junction. At one time it was thought that the entire route west of Salisbury might be taken up, but thankfully this did not happen. When this picture was taken the up-side buildings and station house were in excellent condition. *Author*

ning in several parts to and from such places as Plymouth, Padstow, Bude, Ilfracombe, Torrington and Exmouth, each indicated with a destination board on the coach side.

Some of the trains were purely detachments off West of England services at Salisbury or Templecombe. One of my earliest recollections of a journey to or from London is noticing the exodus of passengers from the train to the station buffet at one of these places. I have often wondered since how many passengers actually got served or how many caught the train again. Such stops were usually quite lengthy with considerable parcels traffic to handle and a change of engines at Salisbury. Even so, I never managed to drink a cup of tea without either burning my mouth or wasting some. China cups were supplied in those days and many were left under carriage seats; I suppose they eventually found their way back to the refreshment rooms. Another memory is of seeing the bell in each compartment marked 'Attendant' and wondering, if I rang it, how anyone would know to which compartment to come.

Other memories of train journeys in those days are of watching the lineside telephone wires, which rose and fell between posts as the train passed. When a train entered a tunnel passengers would get up out of their seats and close all the windows to prevent smoke and smuts coming in, and we dearly loved to see the dog with its handler come along the corridor shaking the box on his back which contained collecting money for the railwaymen's orphanage.

A through coach for Seaton was detached at Seaton Junction off one of the down Waterloo services and the coach was left in the down platform for the branch engine to collect. The timekeeping of this had to be watched as, if it were late going into Seaton and late back, it might well delay an up train.

The Express Dairy had a depot for milk, etc, adjoining the up platform at Seaton Junction and milk tanks were sent to London daily. The site had been chosen by the Dairy as there was a constant flow of natural water from Honiton tunnel. There was also a yard on the up side with long sidings in which even the longest goods trains could be put away (and there were long freight trains in the area then!).

The station staff consisted of two 'Grade One' porters, who did the office work, and a few 'Grade Two' porters who looked after the transfer of passengers and their luggage to and from the branch train. The staff were warned of the approach of a train by means of a platform bell operated by the signalman, and they took their places along the platform to wait on passengers. Some porters would, quite unofficially, carry passengers' cases to

Seaton Junction from the south-west. Note the complex trackwork and signalling. On the left of the picture is the Express Dairy depot. No sidings are in use today. ***Author***

their homes if they lived nearby. The managers knew that this went on but turned a blind eye provided that they were not gone too long from the station. No doubt they were rewarded by the owners of the cases!

Staff were always busy even in the smallest stations - in the winter unloading coal from a wagon for station use, sawing up sleeper wood for kindling fires, in addition to cleaning signal lamps, shunting and station cleaning. There was always tidying up to be done in the goods yard, returning ropes and wagon sheets and cleaning out wagons and cattle pens. In snowy and foggy weather a member of staff was posted to the distant signal and would place a detonator on the rail if the signal was showing a caution aspect. The introduction of colour light signalling many years later greatly reduced the workload (although by then the station had closed). The porters were also responsible for attaching and detaching the through coach for the Seaton branch to and from the London train.

There were two signalmen and a porter signalman; the latter worked a few hours in the box and the remainder of his turn on the platform. The box was a large one on the 'country end' of the down platform (just beyond the buffet which adjoined the waiting rooms).

The signalling was standard three-position block for the main line and a Tyers tablet instrument for the Seaton branch. I can still visualise going up into the box at Seaton Junction where the signalman would have his old dog at his feet in the immaculate surroundings, the levers polished daily and handled with a duster to prevent rust. The tablet instruments rather reminded me of a chocolate machine (which was part of the furniture of most stations) with its drawer from which was produced the tablet for the single line by pulling the handle at the side. This was placed in a leather pouch for carrying purposes.

In a nutshell, for those unfamiliar with it, the principle of single line electric token/tablet working is this. The signalman at No 1 box offers the train to the signalman at No 2 box by the appropriate bell code; the latter repeats it if he can accept the train, and holds in the plunger on his Tyers instrument on the last beat of the code, enabling

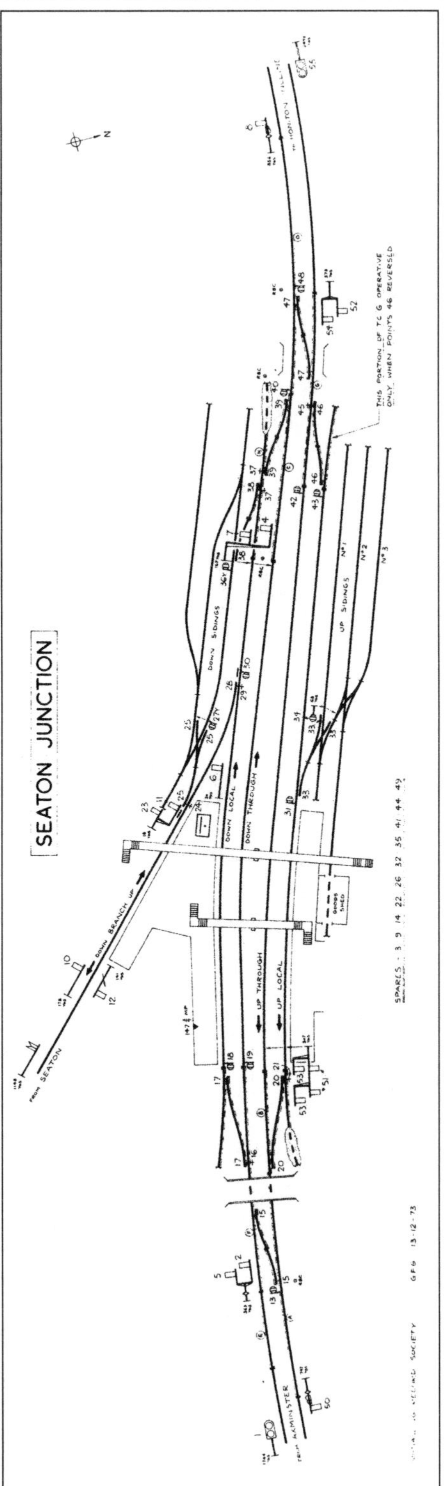

The track and signalling layout at Seaton Junction. *Signalling Record Society*

the signalman at No 1 box to remove a tablet from his machine, which he then gives to the driver. A 'Train Entering Section' signal is given by bell and the train departs. No tablet can be removed from the box at either end of the section until the one in use has been placed in the machine at No 2 box and the appropriate bell signals exchanged. This was an excellent system and there were few collisions on single lines over the years.

In those days the branch train was composed of a two-coach gated set; it was not uncommon to see rain water filling the bowls over the electric light bulbs. It is such a pity that there is so little very old coaching stock preserved. This type of stock was also common on other such branches in those days. The engine on the Seaton branch was an '02' 0-4-4 Adams tank, push-and-pull fitted, which stayed the night at Seaton and changed each Saturday with a fresh engine from Exmouth Junction. There were two guards and two pairs of enginemen who worked the branch, but on summer Sundays (when there was a service) an 'M7' would come out from Exeter with a set of coaches to operate the service and made nonsense of the timetable because of its superior power. On weekdays it was not unusual to see the loco sandwiched between the two-set and a van or the London coach.

There were sidings at Colyton, the first stop on the line, but not at Colyford, where there was a level crossing. When that station was unstaffed, the train crew would stop the train, open the gates, move the train through, and shut the gates behind them. Seaton station was also of quite modern design and had two platforms on one island, the one in general use longer than the other.

Householders living near the railway would wave to trains as they went by and when we returned years later I was amazed to see one of our old friends waving to us in the train. How did she know I would be in that train, I thought in my naive way, never realising that she waved to everyone.

As boys, we spent endless hours in the garden watching the trains. The goods trains were usually hauled by an 'S15' or 'U' Class loco, and stone trains to and from Meldon

A Seaton train in the 'branch' platform. This picture was taken possibly in the 1960s when Maunsell push-and-pull coaches were in use. *Lens of Sutton*

Seaton station. Platform 1 was used for most trains; the other was shorter and to the right of the picture. Like Seaton Junction, this station had a very short life in its rebuilt form, and no trace exists today. *Lens of Sutton*

Colyton, the first station on the branch after Seaton Junction, and a considerable walk from the town it nominally served. *Lens of Sutton*

Colyton in 1987, now the terminus of the narrow gauge Seaton & District Electric Tramway. In appearance it is still much as it was when the railway existed. *Author*

Colyford level crossing in 1987, with a tram crossing the Exeter-Lyme Regis road. The gentlemen's toilet is the only remaining building on the platform. *Author*

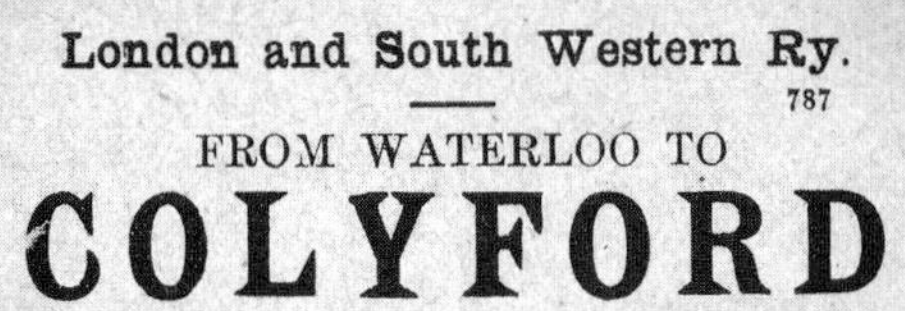

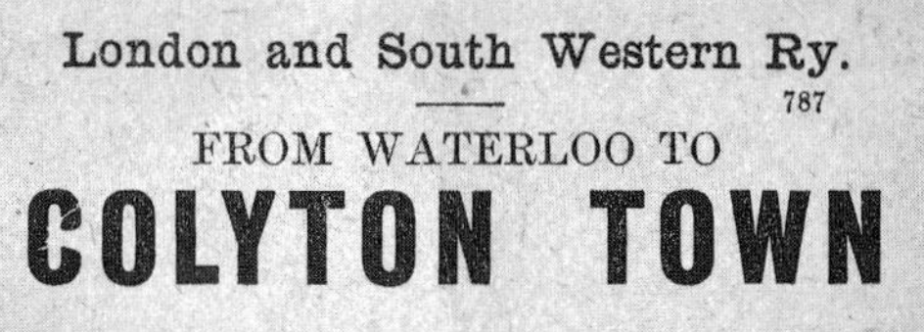

Drummond 'M7' Class 0-4-4 tank No 30670 at Sidmouth. Engines of this class were sometimes used on the Seaton branch. *Real Photographs*

'West Country' Class 'Pacific' No 34017 *Ilfracombe* on Honiton bank. The steep gradient - mostly 1 in 80 - brought out the best in drivers and locos! *Real Photographs*

Quarry near Okehampton were a daily sight. Passenger trains were pulled by a 'King Arthurs' or a smaller mixed traffic tender engine. We would stand in the garden with our hands over our ears while the engines blew off steam after the hard slog over Honiton summit. I always felt that the name of the intermediate box, Honiton Incline, was rather an understatement considering the fact that Honiton bank must surely rank as one of the steepest on such a heavily graded line. In fact, we knew the locos so well that we could often give the engine number before it appeared, just by its sound. As far as I can recollect, coaches on the main line were Maunsell vehicles on which the door handles had to be turned to the horizontal position from outside.

People often ask what the responsibilities of the station master are. In the period of which I write they were rather different from now. In the main, the SM was responsible for the general supervision of the signal box, platform and office, ie for staffing, rostering, discipline, workload and calculation of pay; dealing with travel facilities for staff; commercial matters relating to ticket, parcels and goods accounts; reporting irregularities in ticket matters and operating practices; dealing with claims and refunds from the public; and ordering stationery, stores and uniform (clothing coupons had to be collected from staff during rationing, and red ties were issued so that they could be taken off and used as a danger signal if required).

The SM also dealt with correspondence relating to train service and stock working changes, publicity, enquiries from the public, ensuring that emergency equipment (eg fire-fighting and first aid equipment) was kept in working order and, in some cases, banking of cash and collecting of pay from the bank if there was one nearby.

On pay day my father would meet a certain up train, on which the paymaster would be locked in a compartment for security, to collect the station wages (a practice which would be condemned nowadays).

A copy of an important document in the ticket office was taken by writing in violet copying ink and then placing the document between the leaves of a tissue paper book with damp pages. A heavy press was screwed down overnight and hopefully a clear copy was obtained.

In those days station masters had to wait until they were offered promotion and of course it was foolish to decline a move as it could be some years before a further offer was made. It meant moving house, etc, but that was the understanding when one went into the grade. Thus it was that in May 1939 we all packed up and moved to Petersfield, 17 miles from Portsmouth.

In Southern days, 'King Arthur' Class 4-6-0 No 456 *Sir Galahad* passes Milborne Port between Templecombe and Sherborne. This loco gave its name to my father's Hillman (see opposite). *Real Photographs*

2.
PETERSFIELD 1939-44
The Southern at war

By now my father had acquired a small car, a Hillman; its registration number was 456 so it was named 'Sir Galahad' after the 'King Arthur' Class engine of that name. I have a vague recollection of moving. The furniture went into a container mounted on a flat railway truck and the garden and general items were loaded in a box truck. We stayed the first night en route at Southampton and had the greatest difficulty in starting the car in the morning (a practice which was all too common with this vehicle).

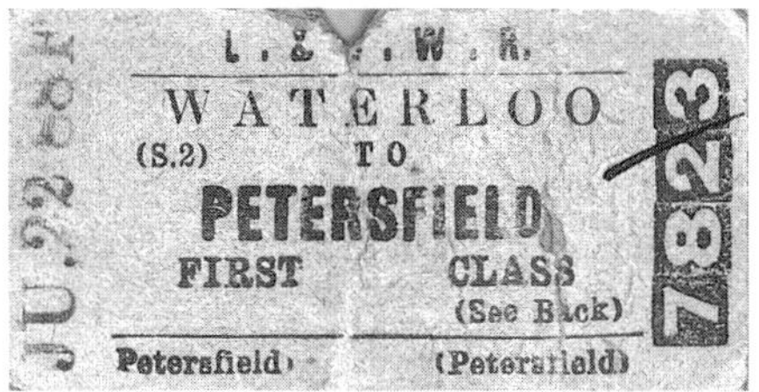

The new life at Petersfield was such a contrast to that at Seaton Junction - a pleasant market town instead of a hamlet, but a very high rambling house lit by gas in contrast to our old home which we had come to love. The only garden was on the up side behind the coal yard, about 10 minutes walk away. It was almost a field, with dozens of apple and pear trees, a small wood with hazelnuts and a stream running through. Naturally trespassing was a problem, but with so much produce I suppose we hardly noticed any losses. My father must have spent every spare minute in the garden either digging, planting or cutting the grass. Of course, for us boys and our friends it was a marvellous playground with trees to climb and streams to bridge, but I cannot remember getting seriously hurt although often very wet and dirty. If we went alone we did not cross the track but used a path adjoining the coal yard.

My parents must have been put to a lot of hard work both after moving and subsequently; with two flights of stairs and long passageways, carpeting and linoleum was, no doubt, an expensive proposition and hard work to lay. Cleaning was difficult because of the size of the house and, of course, there were no labour-saving devices, although with few steam trains there was not quite so much dust about. Shutters for the windows had to be provided as soon as war was declared. This meant saving oddments of wood or using heavy curtains or black paper in addition.

Although there was only a sitting room, dining room and kitchen downstairs, they were separated by a passageway with a right-angled corner in it, and beyond the kitchen was a conservatory leading out to a back yard. A cellar led off the passageway and my father's office was joined to our house by a communicating door. His office was lit by electric light, as was the station, but our house only had gas; the pressure was so poor that it was difficult to see and even harder to get a hot bath from the old-fashioned gas geyser! The bathroom and two bedrooms were on the first floor and a further two bedrooms at the top. As the war progressed we closed off the top storey and used one top bedroom purely for our Hornby model railway layout. It is amazing in these enlightened days when many houses have central heating to look back to the old days when we would

The front of the station in 1988 - it has changed little over the years. Bars were placed over the upstairs windows to prevent little boys from falling out! *Author*

say 'I will light a coal fire in one room to air the house'. Some hopes!

The international situation was worsening and, understandably, my parents were worried about us all, so my brother, my grandparents and I were packed off back to Devon to stay at a delightful cottage belonging to a charming lady in a big house about a mile from Seaton Junction.

The 'phoney war' had started but in Devon one scarcely knew that there was a war on. Our parents came down to see us once or twice and we were lucky enough to have a short holiday at Bude, although there were limits on where one could travel. Back at our village, we attended the local school and went on long walks, and my grandfather played cricket with us for hours on end. On one particular day he took us to Seaton on the train and, while we were waiting for the return train, there was an air raid (probably the town's first). Most organisations had their own shelters and Seaton station was no exception. As far as I can recollect, we went down some steps under the signal box and, after a lot of commotion, heard a plane crash in the river adjoining.

After a few months had elapsed my brother and I went back to Petersfield as the war had not really 'taken off' as expected. When the blitz began we invariably slept in the cellar. I think I can still smell potatoes, paraffin and all the other things which were stored there. Hardly a perfect bedroom! It is surprising how life continued despite one disturbed night after another. We were really very fortunate as we were amongst people that we knew all the time, unlike some of the evacuees that we met who arrived with labels round their necks, taken out of their usual environment and moved from pillar to post wondering where they were going to be put next.

Those adults not called up were either in

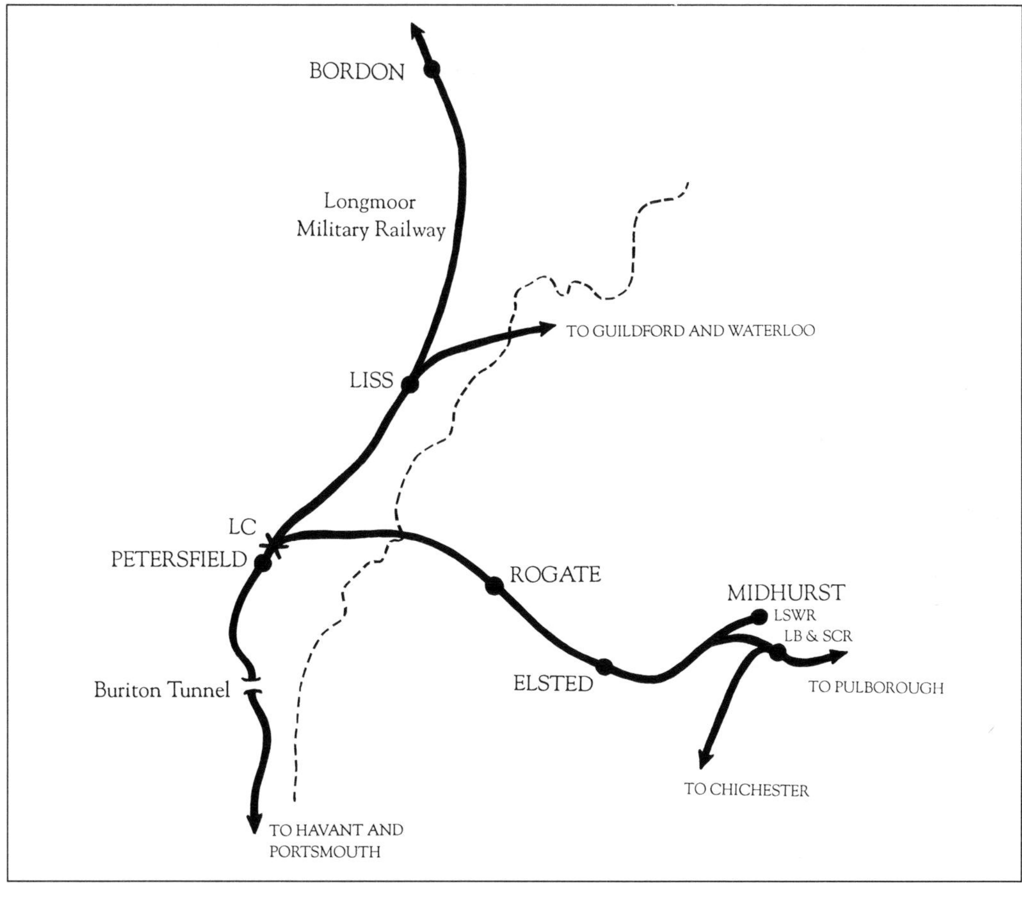

Lines around Petersfield. ***Christina Siviter***

the Auxiliary Fire Service, or a 'Special' in the police force or the Home Guard, or were 'fire watching'; yet people were still at work the next day after being up part of the night. There was fortunately little bomb damage near us but there was an alert night after night; planes could be heard droning overhead and the sky was as bright as day over Portsmouth, which suffered badly. Naturally the train service was affected when the track was hit, cancellations were made to enable more goods trains to run and pathways were reserved for troop trains. In some cases passenger trains were withdrawn for economy reasons, and passengers were being recommended by advertisements on stations and in carriages not to travel unless it was really necessary.

Portsmouth Harbour station was badly damaged and, when eventually it was reopened, one platform alone was usable and was used mainly by Waterloo expresses. Station lights were severely dimmed - blue bulbs being used outdoors and also signs facing roadways were taken down. (I was sorry to see the name 'Petersfield Junction' taken off the signal box. At 'black out' time, station staff would ensure that all blinds were drawn in compartments before a train was allowed to continue. It is surprising that there were comparatively few accidents that could be attributed to the black out.

Petersfield was situated quite close to several army camps - Bordon, Longmoor, etc - so numerous servicemen and women would come to the town in the evenings for entertainment, as would sailors from Portsmouth and Gosport and from inshore establishments nearby. As a child I cannot remember any noise or disturbances at night, but my parents often mentioned high jinks. On one particular night a contest was apparently staged between two regiments, and men were seen swimming fully clothed in one of the static water tanks which had been constructed at strategic points in the town.

In some ways station masters' lives were similar to those of policemen or clergymen - they were well known in the neighbourhood and were never off duty, so people called at the house at all hours with problems. Also one tended to make friends within the business and, when living 'over the shop', it was inevitable that the family felt involved in events, happenings, calamities, etc. For instance, one Saturday afternoon a member of the staff called at the door looking for my father to say that one of the goods porters had been knocked over during shunting and had subsequently died. There were of course minor derailments in the yard from time to time but, fortunately, none of a serious nature.

As our living room backed on to the down platform and was side-on to the ticket office, the actions of the staff became familiar to us. One of the clerks always kept up such a good fire in the office that our wall was always warm from it, whilst another had a habit of scraping his chair along the floor each time he stood up - so we always knew who was on duty! Tickets were stamped up overnight and this could be clearly heard from the house - they were dated by means of a dating press that put just a date on one end of a single ticket, or at both ends of return tickets. Such presses survived well into the 1960s, when the cash register took over. A variation on

Portsmouth Harbour station on 13 August 1940 after the blitz. For a period of time only one platform was used, most trains terminating at Portsmouth & Southsea. ***National Railway Museum, York***

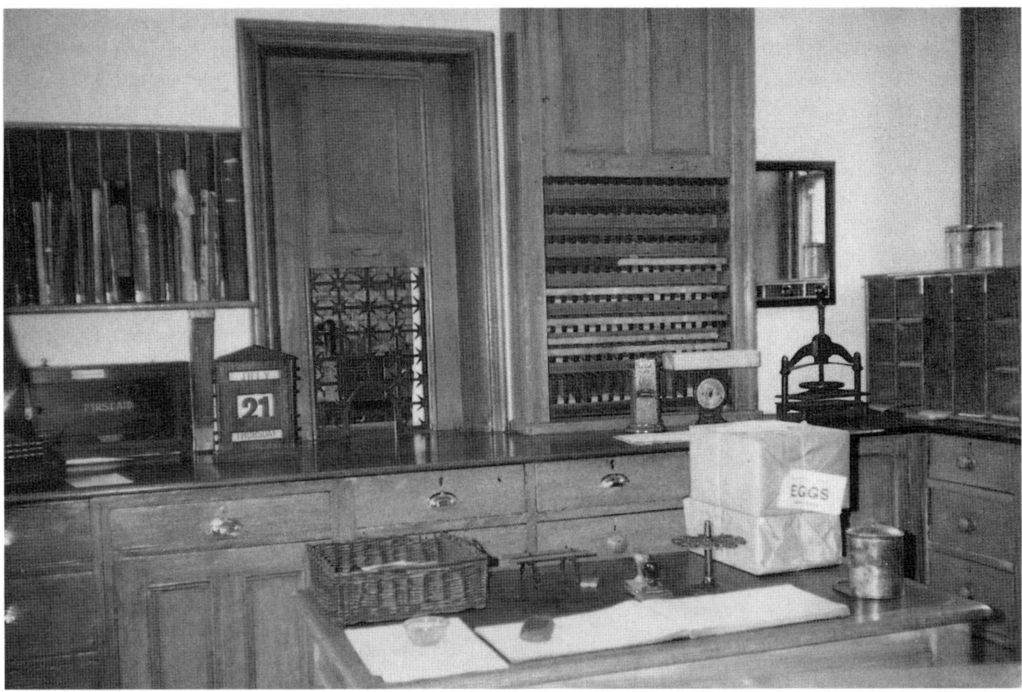

A typical ticket office interior with dating press and 'gravity feed' tubes. This example is preserved at the North of England Open Air Museum, Beamish. ***Author***

the theme of nosey neighbours!

It was interesting to watch the porters rolling milk churns along the platform. Some were skilled enough to roll a churn with each hand, a knack never exercised nowadays. (In case anyone does not know how this is done, the churn is tilted slightly from the vertical and, if only one is being rolled, one hand is passed over the other to move the churn along. If two are rolled together the same method is adopted but momentarily the hand in question has to be lifted off the churn to get a grip further round while the other hand rolls another in the same way.)

For a while a lady booking clerk lodged with us as she lived away and could not get to the station for the 'early turn', so she was able to see life from 'our side of the wall'.

1940 was one of the worst winters for many years and telephone wires were down for miles around. This was the only time that I remember seeing steam engines haul electric trains, as the latter had difficulty in picking up the current. It was not until the 1980s that we experienced similar conditions, when diesel-electric locos assisted electric trains.

Another practice which is no longer carried out is the discharging of the traction current at night, since of course freight trains at night were all steam-hauled then.

As schools and individual evacuees moved to Petersfield from London and Portsmouth it meant that we could only go to school part-time, the evacuees using the school for the remainder of the day. Extra free time no doubt gave us lads more time to get up to mischief, but I do not recall any vandalism occurring or us getting into serious trouble. Nonetheless, as the station subway was side-on to our back yard, passengers going up or down the steps must have wondered why they got wet, unable to see the lads positioned with water pistols against the holes in the roof! However, when the victim was the book-stall manager the truth came out, as he had met us before! I suppose my father must have been rather embarrassed at times.

We had a lucky escape on one occasion;

while we were playing in a truck of sacks, the hinged wagon door burst open, throwing us and the sacks out on to the off side of the siding. Fortunately no one was hurt. Saturday afternoon became our favourite time for 'using' the goods yard as it was normally deserted, and it was on such a day that we found a 'pinch bar' (used for moving railway wagons by levering the wheels) and actually moved a wagon about a hundred yards. Naturally no one blamed us, as how could a few young boys move a large railway truck all that way? Little did we realise the extreme folly of so doing - the result could possibly have been a serious crash.

In those days almost all goods sold by shops came by rail, and another pastime which could be indulged in a little at a time was the unloading of empty lemonade bottles from a crate at the station and taking them back to the shop for the penny to be refunded. We were, however, inclined to get too greedy and the shopkeeper became suspicious.

I became very friendly with the horse delivery man, Mr Bristow, and often went out with him on his deliveries, marvelling at the way the old horse knew at which shops to stop without having to be told. In the evenings we would go down to the stables to bed the horse down and feed him. Here were problems again which would not obtain today. When the carter wanted a day or weekend off a member of the platform staff had to look after the horse, and very few were anxious to undertake this. From time to time the stables which were rented became unavailable and someone had to look round for new premises.

Most of the staff were very friendly and spent quite a bit of time with us. It is surprising how many railwaymen were also tradesman, and on several occasions they did jobs for us - there were gardeners, car mechanics, cabinet-makers, clock-menders, to name but a few.

We all had bikes and we were fortunate in having the goods yard handy in which to learn to cycle. How my father ever prevented my brother Ray from riding off the edge of the 'dock' I shall never know - he ran about 300 yards in no time at all, just in time to

'700' Class 0-6-0 No 316 near Petersfield with an apology for a goods train! *Real Photographs*

stop him disappearing over the edge on to the track.

Trips to the countryside were frequent, as such lovely scenery could be found on the Hants/Sussex/Surrey border which was not to be missed. On one occasion my brother and I found ourselves in the Longmoor area and, whilst looking about, and waving to soldiers, we suddenly found ourselves in a ditch with the front cycle wheel badly buckled as a result of getting it stuck in the railway lines. I then gave a sob story to the signalman at Longmoor signal box (on the Military Railway) who allowed us to travel to Liss and thence to Petersfield.

Travel on the Longmoor Military Railway was free but at one's own risk. This railway was not new to us as we would visit the station master at Bordon from time to time, and the nearest way from Petersfield was via Liss and the LMR. Although he was only in charge of the SR station, no doubt he was closely involved with the LMR and knew most of the officers pretty well.

(8/44) **SOUTHERN RAILWAY.**

(787)

FROM WATERLOO TO

BORDON

Station masters' evening and weekend duties were shared with the man at the next station on an 'on call' arrangement and so, if he went out, the address or telephone number where he was had to be made available were he to be needed. Dad also had responsibility for Buriton Sidings, and unless he could travel down on a goods train the only access was by road. A visit was organised one day with an Inspector to accompany him and they decided by go by car and asked me if I would like to go too; but at the last minute the Inspector was unable to come. On the way back a lorry collided with our car and did untold damage to the rear. Luckily as there were only the two of us travelling I was sitting in the front and escaped with cuts and a few stitches. I feel that I owe my life to that man (whoever he was) since had he been there I would most certainly have been put in the back seat, and who knows what the result would have been?

It is difficult to imagine how busy most of the Southern Railway goods yards were.

Bordon station - the military station was only a few yards away. 'M7' 0-4-4s - this is No 30027 - worked most of the branch lines on the South Western for many years. ***Collector Cards***

An old postcard view of Petersfield station before electrification. In those days the Midhurst train used the up loop platform, but to prevent it having to cross the main line and the busy A272 level crossing to gain the Midhurst line, a new platform was provided on the down side opposite the signal box. *Author's Collection*

A later view of the new unsheltered branch platform, the level crossing and the signal box. *Lens of Sutton*

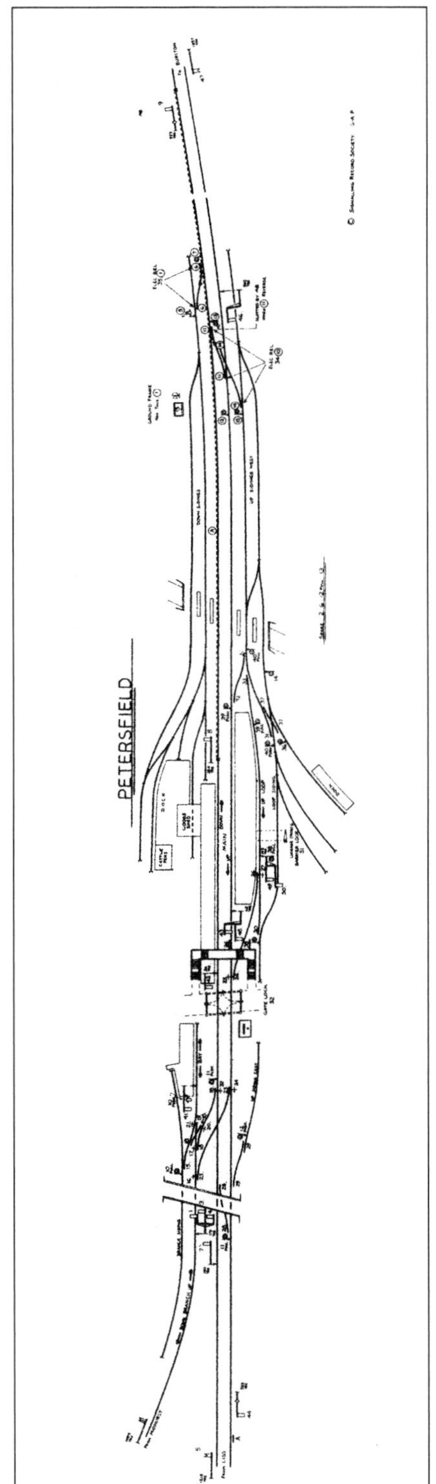

The track and signalling layout at Petersfield. Note the ground frame controlling the connections at the right-hand end of the layout, and the arrangements for the Midhurst branch trains beyond the level crossing. *Signalling Record Society*

Petersfield had a large coal yard on the up side and a goods yard on the down with a ground frame controlling it. There were various shunting turns on weekdays, as four or five different freights came and went daily, most of the shunting being undertaken by a 'Q' Class 0-6-0 or a '700' Class 'Black Motor' (Drummond 0-6-0). We were given a treat on a Saturday when a Guildford 'A12' Adams tender engine would pay us a visit. They certainly looked very ancient.

Petersfield station had rather a unique layout. An up loop platform was provided but with only a trailing connection at the Portsmouth end and not being electrified it was not particularly useful. The loop had been provided for the Midhurst branch, but with electrification of the main line a special wooden structure without buildings was built on the London side of the level crossing on the down side to avoid the gates being opened and to avoid the branch trains crossing and recrossing the main line. These trains ran an irregular service, some terminating at Midhurst whilst others waited there for a while and later continued to Pulborough.

Passengers were never very numerous. Trains were usually push-and-pull and hauled by an 'M7' 0-4-4 tank or a Brighton 'DI' tank with either a 'Brighton' two-coach set with a side corridor but no corridor doors and a sliding guard's door, or LSWR sets with ring-type door handles which had to be turned to the horizontal from outside.

On at least one occasion during the war the branch was used for a troop train reversing at Petersfield. Secondary routes were often used for troop trains and munitions, partly to relieve the overcrowded main lines and partly for safety. They were less likely to be bombed away from large towns and large yards and would often shelter in tunnels.

The Petersfield loop platform was used daily by the milk train, usually hauled by an 'M7' or 'K10', but the Sunday engine was always a 'stranger', usually a 'T14' or 'L12', so although we lived in an electrified area there was no shortage of locos to be seen. There was an hourly fast electric service from Waterloo to Portsmouth and vice versa which did not stop at Petersfield (except dur-

The Midhurst branch

The first station was Rogate for Harting - a long way from both! *Lens of Sutton*

Elsted, looking towards Midhurst. We frequently visited this station as the station house was occupied by a former station master who had given up his retirement to help out at Petersfield during the war. *Lens of Sutton*

Midhurst. Trains were often booked to wait here for a considerable time for a connection from Chichester which had ceased to run many years before. *Real Photographs*

A push-and-pull train leaving Pulborough for Petersfield. *Pamlin Prints*

A 4COR unit waiting to leave Waterloo with a fast train to Portsmouth Harbour. These units maintained the fast Waterloo-Portsmouth service throughout the war whilst 2BIL sets ran the stopping services. The stencil indicator blanking out the left-hand window shows why the units were nicknamed 'Nelsons'. *Real Photographs*

ing the morning and evening peak when they stood over the level crossing and caused some delay to the busy A272 road traffic). The rolling-stock was always a 4COR. (Strangely enough, I never heard the nickname 'Nelsons' used in those days.) The stopping service was invariably a 2BIL but very occasionally a 2NOL and 2HAL would put in an appearance, probably due to stock disruption as a result of enemy action. The main-line signalling was Sykes 'lock and block', while the 'branch' used the Tyers tablet system.

Petersfield was, and still is, served by a variety of bus services, and we had arranged to pay a visit on our cousins which required a bus journey - quite a rarity for us. As buses were infrequent and usually full, we decided to walk to the Square where they started to ensure a seat. Even so there were crowds and my mother and brother and I just managed to get on before the conductor said 'full up'. Dad was left behind and whilst we were wondering what to do, the driver climbed in and started. After a short stop whilst the conductor remonstrated with some others who tried to get on the bus, we were on the move again but could not see father. Apparently his idea was to hurry to the station and persuade the signalman to close the crossing gates across the road, then, whilst the bus was stopped, leap in. His timing was slightly wrong as our bus approached him before he got to the station, but as it took a right turn Dad leapt on like an athlete. I do not know whether the conductor did not see him or simply turned a blind eye, but he stayed on the vehicle and so we continued on an otherwise uneventful day.

The outside station staff at Petersfield consisted of two signalmen, two porter signalmen, two foremen, two parcels porters and two Grade Two porters. There were no ticket collectors, but the parcels porters would leave the parcels office every 15 minutes to attend to the barrier, as the up trains were evenly spaced between the downs, although a few hours were missed and the service waxed and waned throughout the war. In the goods yard were two shunters, a checker, a motor driver, a horse driver, and various goods porters and clerks.

Signal lamps were the responsibility of a lamp boy who spent the entire week on this task. In addition to walking up to Liss, changing and cleaning signal lamps at the crossings (Kings Fernsden, Sheet, Stodham and Princes' Bridge), out on the Midhurst branch a short way and through Buriton tunnel to Rowlands Castle, he performed platform duties in his spare time. Perhaps it is a good thing that a boy of 14 is not expected to do such a job now, especially in the electrified area. As might be expected, some of the lads were not the most eloquent or the greatest scholars, and my father was very amused when one of the boys gave in his notice to leave on the back of a wagon label and finished by saying 'Kind regards to your family'; another asked for a day's leave to go to weeding (it transpired that he wished to attend a wedding!).

I think the only time that my father refused promotion was during the war when the authorities offered him a station master's post at Portland. It was considered bad form to turn down a higher grade, but when they told him that the station had been blitzed and several members of the staff killed, understandably he declined the offer. Possibly the future of the entire family would have been very different had he taken it.

My father bought me a book as a present one day and this was the first time that I had ever seen engine numbers listed in classes published with pictures. This seemed too marvellous for words as previously I had either memorised what locos I had seen or listed them in a notebook, so I set to work marking off the book. Imagine my surprise when soon after I had been given the book I saw an ugly monstrosity of an engine which was not listed, and which looked as though it had been built of scrap iron and indeed not finished. I refer, of course, to Bulleid's 'Q1' Class. It is a pity that we cannot appreciate the everyday things of life; it is only when we wake up one day and suddenly realise that something no longer exists that we wish we knew more about it and had taken more notice at the time.

3.
SITTINGBOURNE 1944-49
North Kent interlude

My father was beginning to think that he was due for another move and there was considerable speculation as to where it might be, bearing in mind that he knew who was due for retirement. We enjoyed the thought of exploring yet another new place, but leaving our friends was a bit of a wrench. Although all sorts of promises were made, there were very few friends with whom I was able to keep in touch, and it took quite a while to settle each time we moved.

My father knew Hampshire very well as he had been brought up in Southampton and had been in the booking office at Liss many years before becoming a station master, but when his next promotion came along in 1944 it was to an area of which the family had no previous knowledge - Sittingbourne, in the London East Division; in my ignorance I had not even realised that Kent was part of the Southern Railway.

1st - SINGLE SINGLE - 1st
Sittingb'rne & Milton Regis to
Sittingbourne Blackfriars or Victoria
BLACKFRIARS or VICTORIA
Via Chatham
(S) 11/3 FARE 11/3 (S)
For condit'ns see over For condit'ns see over

A 1st single from Sittingbourne to Victoria, dating from the late 'fifties.

The war was by no means over, although things were looking better and some of the restrictions regarding the black out were being lifted. However, only a few weeks earlier our new area had been in the news when a flying bomb had exploded under a bridge between Rainham and Newington just as a busy train was approaching. Although the driver made an emergency brake application he was unable to stop, but despite the fact that the train was very full, casualties were comparatively light.

This area of Kent still had black out restrictions, so in that respect it was going to be a backward step. A preview of our future home was called for, so one Sunday we worked out our trains to go down to Sittingbourne for the day to measure up for curtains, linoleum, etc. It was also a retrograde step in that we were going back to steam trains again, which we realised when we tried to work out our service to go and get back in the same day, bearing in mind that the Sunday service was even worse than a the weekday one, with 3 hours between trains on occasions. Our journey down was from Waterloo Junction (as my parents always called it), changing at Chatham into a down Victoria service.

The first thing we noticed was the effects of the war around North West Kent. Having been used to open countryside, the contrast was very noticeable, with the view from the train being mainly factories, derelict sites and packed roads of small terraced houses split up by bombed buildings and shops; I am sure that my parents must have had second thoughts. After only an hour to examine our new house it was time to catch the train back to Victoria, which proved to be a more attractive route with orchards and open countryside much of the way.

After moving in, the first task we had was

Oak Lane, Newington, after enemy action on 16 August 1944. The 3.35 pm Victoria-Ramsgate was crossing the bridge as the V1 rocket exploded below. ***National Railway Museum, York***

to make hurriedly some black out shutters for our windows. By torchlight we measured the shutters we already had and realised that they were marginally too big, so a piece had to be sawn off. On applying them to the windows we found that we had mis-measured in the dark and had to fix the piece back on again.

The house was lit by gas (as was the station) and comprised a kitchen and scullery downstairs, and four bedrooms, a bathroom with a sink and a sitting room and dining room upstairs. The largest room was the bathroom in which one could easily accommodate a grand piano with room to spare. The bath was mounted on small legs, making it rather high, and we were told that our predecessors had it disconnected each winter to prevent freezing. I suppose they did not bathe when it was cold. We had small oil heaters in some of the rooms to take the chill off.

In the kitchen downstairs was an old range, and my mother would make the most delicious soup by collecting all the scraps of meat and bones left over and letting them simmer for the entire weekend.

Outside the kitchen and scullery was a small back yard about 6 feet square with high walls where mother dried her washing and a toilet in one corner, illuminated by a noisy gas lamp which burned with a fish-tail flame (before gas mantles were used).

Of course we had no telephone in the house, so if any calls came for us either a member of the staff had to fetch us or, if we were expecting a call, we would wait in the office. As most of my mother's family were in Canada, you can imagine the problem - invariably by the time we got to the telephone the call had been disconnected, or we waited for hours on end for a call which did not come.

The station was covered by an overall sloping roof and as the house windows were not high enough to see over it, the outlook was purely the slope of the roof. The layout of the station has not changed much over the years but there was a subway in addition to the overbridge, and a buffet was provided on both sides. The down side refreshment room was not in use and the windows were very dirty; it was common knowledge that troops had their own keys and slept in it. The Royal Navy was well represented, as dockyards were situated at Chatham and Sheerness, so often there was fun and games in the late evening after the public houses closed. The last Sheerness service was at 11.30 pm, so it was not unusual for sailors to spend at least an hour on the station premises.

The Sheerness branch train was almost invariably a three-coach SE&CR set of the 'birdcage' variety hauled by an 'R1' or 'H' Class 0-4-4 tank, but was not push-and-pull operated. Saturday afternoons sometimes saw a turnover engine, often a 'C' Class 0-6-0, the same class which hauled most of the local goods trains. Daily (including certain Sundays) an 'O1' Class 0-6-0 was provided as a shunting pilot. Most of the time the attaching and detaching of the Sheerness branch engine was performed by the platform porters. We always considered the SE&CR men to be excellent shunters - the attaching of a loco was rarely felt by the passengers, unlike in some other parts of the country where one would be only too aware of the

Sittingbourne station looking east. Note the overall roof and the gas lamps. ***Real Photographs***

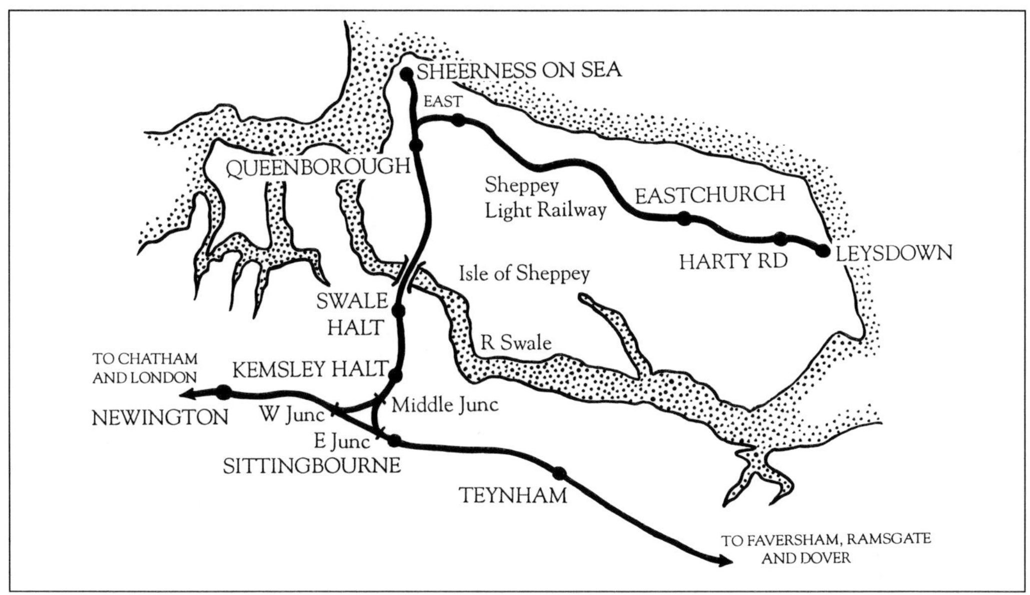

Lines around Sittingbourne and the Isle of Sheppey. ***Christina Siviter***

engine being attached.

There has never been a frequent service to or from Sheerness by the western spur of the triangle but a few trains ran to and from Chatham at irregular times and for a period there was a Sheerness-Victoria train at about noon on Saturdays. There were also a few Chatham-Sheerness trains via Sittingbourne and vice versa, reversing in the down loop platform at the latter. An up starting signal was provided to start trains from the down loop but it was not and still is not reversible at the country end.

My parents were always very keen on walking and so, as my father was 'on call', Sunday evenings were usually spent in taking the train to Kemsley Halt and walking back. The route of our walk was close to the railway triangle, so Dad could see if anything was amiss. But as Sunday trains were so few and far between we were usually home in time for the next one.

The main-line service was not terribly frequent either and was often the subject of newspaper articles. The early morning services to Cannon Street were three in number; in later years one of these ran fast from Whitstable to Cannon Street and reduced Sittingbourne's up Cannon Street services to two (one of which started from Herne Bay), the first up Victoria service being 09.05. There was not a regular up service, but in most cases Teynham, Newington and Rainham were served by a Faversham-Chatham shuttle service in each direction. In the down direction there was a departure from Victoria at 35 minutes past most hours in the off-peak time. During the evening peak all down services started from Cannon Street; one of these divided at Chatham with a Sheerness portion. For quite a few years after electrification the new service from Cannon Street to Ramsgate/Dover bore a considerable similarity to the steam service and the down Victoria service was at 40 minutes past most hours.

I will not try to list the entire service since in most years minor alterations took place, and other publications do this with greater detail. A few gaps were plugged over the years and certain services were accelerated by cutting out stops. As I have already said, the Sunday service had gaps of 3 hours without trains and the station was locked up at midday and late afternoon between trains.

Motive power was provided by a variety of

Main Lines (via North Kent and Chatham)—*continued.*

Timing Number	—		—		—		—		—				—				—	
UP TRAINS. SUNDAYS.			Vans.				10.14 a.m. Chatham.											
	a.m.		a.m.		a.m.		a.m.		a.m.				a.m.				a.m.	
	arr.	dep.	arr.	dep.	arr.	dep.	arr.	dep.	arr.	dep.			arr.	dep.			arr.	dep.
RAMSGATE														9 40				
Dumpton Pk. (for E. Ramsgate)													9 43	9 44				
Broadstairs													9 47	9 49				
Margate East																		
MARGATE													9 55	9 58				
Westgate-on-Sea													10 2	10 3				
Birchington													10 7	10 8				
Herne Bay				9 30									10 20	10 22				
Chestfield & Swalecliffe Halt																		
Whitstable & Tankerton													10 29	10 31				
Faversham													10 41					
DOVER Marine																		
DOVER Priory										9 42								
Kearsney									9 47	9 48								
Stonehall & Lydden Halt																		
Shepherd's Well									9 55	9 56								
Snowdown & Nonington Halt									10 0	10 1								
Aylesham Halt									10 3	10 4								
Adisham									10 7	10 8								
Bekesbourne									10 13	10 14								
Canterbury East									10 20	10 21								
Selling									10 33	10 34								
FAVERSHAM			9	50		10 10			10 40					10 46				
Teynham					10 18	10 19												
SITTINGBOURNE		9 47	10	3	10 25	10 26							10 57	10 59				11 10
Eastern Junction	9	48															11	11
Middle Junction	9	49					10	31									11	12
Kemsley Halt	9 52	9 53					10 34	10 35									11 15	11 16
Swale Halt																		
Queenborough	9 59½	10 0½					10 42	10 43									11 22½	11 23½
SHEERNESS-ON-SEA	10 5						10 48										11 28	
Western Junction																		
Newington					10 32	10 33												
Rainham					10 38	10 39												
Gillingham (Kent)			10 15	10 35	10 44	10 45												
CHATHAM			10	38	10 49								11 13	11 15				
Rochester																		
Rochester Bridge Junction			10	41									11	17½				
STROOD																		
Higham																		
GRAVESEND CENTRAL																		
DARTFORD																		
Erith																		
WOOLWICH ARSENAL																		
Greenwich																		
Sole Street			10	57									11	31				
Meopham																		
Fawkham																		
Farningham Road																		
SWANLEY			11	10									11	41				
St. Mary Cray																		
Bickley Junction													11	47				
Bickley																		
Bromley South													11 50	11 52				
Shortlands																		
Shortlands Junction													11	54½				
BECKENHAM JUNCTION																		
HERNE HILL																		
Chislehurst			11	16														
Hither Green Junction			11	22														
New Cross			11	26														
LONDON BRIDGE																		
CANNON STREET			To R. Road arrive 11.35 a.m.															
WATERLOO																		
CHARING CROSS																		
NUNHEAD													12	2				
BLACKFRIARS																		
HOLBORN VIADUCT																		
VICTORIA													12 13					

'Schools' Class No 939 *Leatherhead* at Aylesford. These locos hauled many of the Kent Coast trains via Chatham, and were very popular with drivers because of their quick acceleration. *Lens of Sutton*

ex-SE&CR locos, 'F1', 'E1', 'D1', 'L1', etc - sometimes a 'U1' and a few 'King Arthurs' and 'Schools'. I would try and arrange to see some of the down evening Cannon Street services as a 'rarer' 'Schools' could be seen. Some of these trains ran to Dover, so a Dover-based loco would be in charge. I have always been a keen admirer of the 'Schools' and most of them looked immaculate and were a joy to watch when pulling away without any slipping or setting back when starting. Almost every day the 09.45 Ramsgate-Victoria would be hauled by No 922 *Marlborough* and the service was always known as the 'Granville' after a train which had run many years before over this route. This engine was shining even at a time when the others were not cleaned so well, and it returned on the front of the 3.35 pm Victoria-Ramsgate.

One of the evening up trains started from Ashford whilst another originated from Folkestone Central (no doubt several of the trains were 'rounders', ie Charing Cross-Ramsgate-Victoria, so why not show them as such in the timetable?). The last up weekday service ran to Charing Cross via Woolwich and I would try hard to stay awake to hear the staff call out the unusual-sounding station names.

Summer Saturdays and Sundays produced some unusual services; some of the coaching stock was very ancient and almost every available loco was brought into use. These started from New Cross, Maze Hill, Blackheath and other such unlikely spots (close to carriage sidings), and I well remember seeing 'T9' 4-4-0s in use for a season for two.

Sittingbourne goods yard was very busy, despatching a considerable amount of fruit traffic in season together with paper from the local mills and livestock from the town market in addition to the usual merchandise.

Left **Part of the Working Timetable for the line through Sittingbourne in 1947. Note the long periods between trains, and entries for Margate East and Stonehall & Lydden Halt, closed in 1953 and 1954 respectively. Note also the Herne Bay to Rotherhithe Road van train (second column). All light engine movements and parcels trains are shown, as are passing times for fast trains at salient points. (Fawkham is now Longfield.) *Author's Collection***

The Sheppey Light Railway

Queenborough station, with 'R1' Class No 31705 in the bay platform on a Sheppey Light Railway train. *Collector Cards*

Eastchurch station, in very rural surroundings. *Real Photographs*

Harty Road Halt, between Eastchurch and Leysdown, in an even more rural setting on 11 March 1950. Guard Bill Gibson is waiting to close the gates after the unidentified 'R1' has passed. *G. W. Gibson*

There were three horse-drawn delivery vehicles and two motors (extra vehicles were provided in the cherry season). Spare trailers were provided so that loading and unloading could be undertaken whilst the carter was out on his rounds, and among the staff were number-takers, messengers, checkers, shunters and head shunters, a yard foreman and several goods porters and clerks.

No public address system was provided but most of the staff had lusty voices and made lengthy announcements, some of which could be heard a long distance away. When the service changed each year, the staff would rule off and post the timetable bills and set up the metal departure indicators which consisted of individual letters and figures slid into a metal board; this task took some days to do bearing in mind that footnotes applied, rather like the present printed posters giving times under each destination. I clearly remember the title over one column said 'St Pauls and Ludgate' - a few years out of date.

There was a branch train service from Queenborough on the Sheppey line to Leysdown (the Sheppey Light Railway) which was usually hauled by an 'R1' with a two-coach articulated set which had been a railmotor with its engine subsequently removed and rebuilt with compartments instead. At school, teachers were strictly told that on no account must boys from Leysdown be allowed to miss the 4.02 pm Sittingbourne-Sheerness as that was the last connection of the day for Leysdown! There were numerous level crossings and the train crew would stop the train, open the gates in front, and stop the train again beyond the crossing to close them. I made one or two journeys on the line but passengers were never numerous. As is so often the case, Leysdown became more popular as a seaside place after the line closed. A bay platform was provided at Queenborough on the Sittingbourne-bound side at the Sheerness end.

Sittingbourne boasted a signal box at each end of the station, Sykes 'lock and block' signalling instruments being in use on the main line. 'A' box (west of Milton Road bridge)

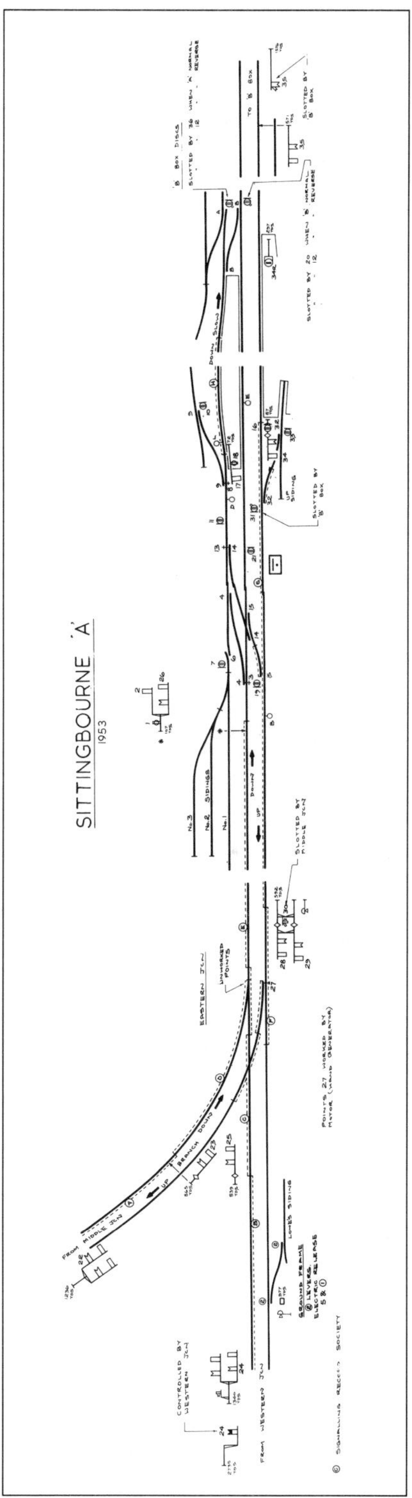

The track and signalling layout at Sittingbourne 'A' box in 1953, controlling the London end of the station and the Eastern Junction corner of the triangular junction. *Signalling Record Society*

The Sittingbourne triangle

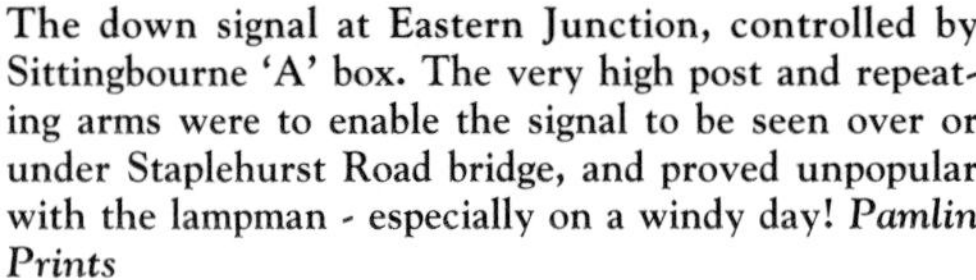

The down signal at Eastern Junction, controlled by Sittingbourne 'A' box. The very high post and repeating arms were to enable the signal to be seen over or under Staplehurst Road bridge, and proved unpopular with the lampman - especially on a windy day! *Pamlin Prints*

Western Junction. Although the conductor rail seems to have been laid, semaphore signalling survives. Note the warning signal at the base of the post to indicate to a train proceeding towards Sheerness that it has been accepted under Regulation 5 ('Section Clear but Station or Junction Blocked'). *Real Photographs*

also controlled the Eastern Junction of the triangle, but separate boxes were provided at Western Junction and Middle Junction (at the apex of the triangle) up to the introduction of the new box at Sittingbourne at the time of the resignalling in the 'fifties.

'B' box controlled the goods yard and was situated close to the present-day panel box. It was here that an 'Annett's key' was kept which was given to drivers who shunted Murston sidings - they used it to release the sidings ground frame and 'lock themselves in' to allow passengers trains to pass whilst they placed their wagons. After shunting, the ground frame was re-locked and the key handed in at Teynham.

Sidings were also provided for Messrs Lowe - makers of animal foods - between Sittingbourne and Western Junction on the up line; after shunting the siding the engine would continue up to Western Junction and, as there was no crossover there, would then reverse on the 'wrong' line to Middle Junction, authorised by the latter's signalman holding a green flag over his head, hoping it could be seen over the fields. As the four lines became one at Middle Junction, the engine could return to Sittingbourne via the eastern side of the triangle on the proper line, and get turned into the bargain. Other engines came to Sittingbourne to turn by this means.

Middle Junction, where the four converging lines became single at the Sheerness corner of the triangle. One solitary Tilley lamp assists the signalman to hand over the single line token. ***Pamlin Prints***

At Middle Junction electric key token instruments were provided for working to Kemsley Halt (where there was a passing loop) or to Queenborough when the former was switched out. I was fascinated to see the signalman at Middle Junction run up and down two flights of stairs on average about once every half-hour to deliver or collect the tablet by the light of a Tilley lamp as the engine passed enveloped in steam at speed. The train had to keep up a good speed as it was not unknown for one to get stuck on the sharp curves, especially with a heavy freight, so the drivers preferred to get a run at it! The signalmen had to be fit in those days.

Water was not provided at the signal boxes, so cans had to be off-loaded daily from a freight train and the empties returned in the same way. In fact, some cottages also had their water delivered in this way. No doubt they used considerably less than the average householder as a result.

Kemsley Halt, the first stop on the Sheerness branch, was reasonably well placed near the village and was fairly busy, unlike Swale Halt, the next station, which quite a few trains missed. Swale Halt was situated on the Sittingbourne side of the river bridge and was never staffed in my time; a notice requested would-be passengers to purchase their tickets at the toll house situated on the bridge. I wonder how many passengers went to this trouble. Then again, I wonder why we do not employ this method more today for unstaffed stations and make the nearest shop or house a sort of travel agent.

My friends would sometimes come with me on a Saturday cycle ride to neighbouring stations. There was a loco shed at Gillingham and Faversham but it was unlikely that we would see anything there that we could not see at home, so a trip further afield

The Sheerness branch

Kemsley Halt, the first crossing place on the single branch beyond Sittingbourne Middle Junction (the line is now double from Sittingbourne to the Swale bridge). In this view, looking towards Sittingbourne, the signal box cum ticket office, since demolished, is on the right, jutting out on to the platform. *Lens of Sutton*

Queenborough station, looking towards Sheerness. *Lens of Sutton*

Platform 1 at Sheerness on Sea, with 'H' Class No 31307 waiting to leave with a 'birdcage' set for Sittingbourne. *Real Photographs*

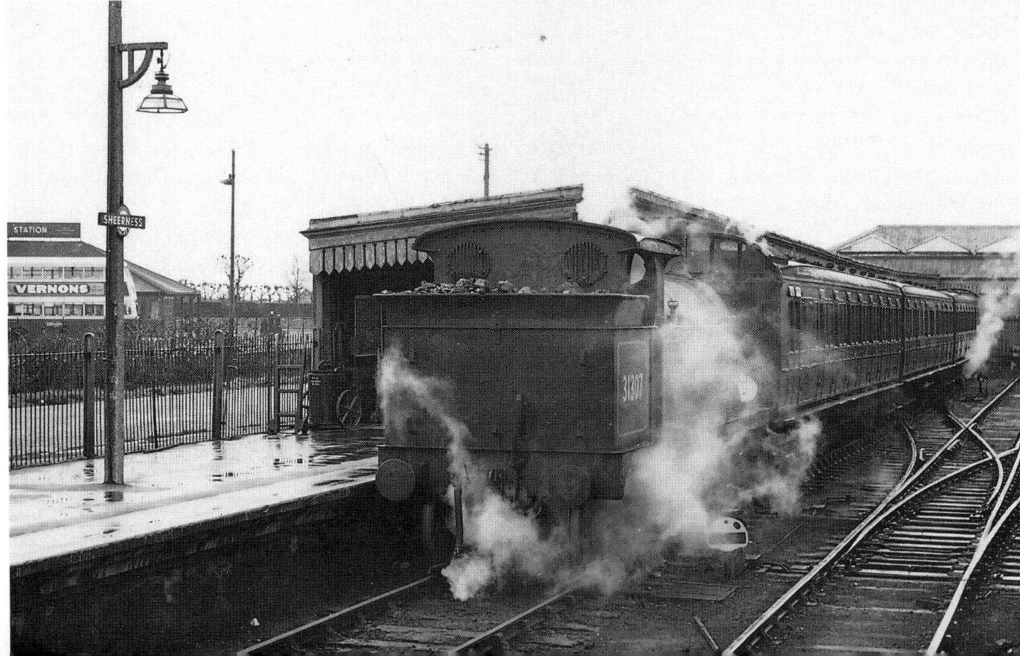

Another view of Sheerness with 'C' Class 0-6-0 No 31584 and an unidentified tank engine on the middle road. ***Lens of Sutton***

was necessary. Hollingbourne was only about 7 miles, and there it was possible to see a 'J' Class tank on a Maidstone-Ashford local. Ashford itself - 20 miles away - was just about possible if we had plenty of time, but what a reward was there on which to feast our eyes!

As the 'dependents' of railway staff, we were entitled to railway privilege tickets and were the envy of all our friends. It was necessary in those days for a privilege application form to be completed by the employee for each journey to be made, and countersigned by the station master. It was difficult for an employee to decide in advance what journeys he would be making to get some 'signed up', but 'owing' privilege orders went on quite a lot, although the auditors objected to it. In addition we were also entitled to a few free tickets each year, so these were reserved for long distances. In later years, station masters and their families were entitled to First Class travel in certain grades, so imagine our delight when a Ticket Inspector attempted to move us from the First Class compartment only to find that we had the appropriate ticket!

Since I went home to dinner from school, I was able to report back in the afternoon to my fellow spotters if anything untoward had happened during the morning, as my father would tell me if fresh locos had appeared. I was quite delighted to hear from him that a 'West Country' Class loco had been seen in the morning and should return in charge of the 3.35 pm Victoria-Ramsgate. Day after day the faithful few turned up after school only to find an 'Arthur' or 'Schools' on the working. After a few days, when I was about to be lynched, our patience was rewarded and, I think, 21C121 was the first 'West Country' I saw on that line. An elderly signalman in 'A' box always referred to the 'West Countries' as 'Southerns' (I suppose he knew that it was one of the points of the compass and was unsure which. Or perhaps the most likely explanation was that the new engines were clean enough to see the word 'Southern' on the tender.)

The electric service from London ran only as far as Maidstone and Gillingham (these were not very popular with the passengers as suburban or 'HAL' stock was used and not quite as comfortable as main-line steam-hauled coaches). There was a plan for electrification in 1948 but this, of course, was shelved; had it materialised it is unlikely that the line from Middle Junction to Swale Bridge would have been doubled. (The old Swale Bridge was still in use in the time of which I am writing - although there was a lot of talk about a new bridge).

The quadrupling of tracks between Rainham and Newington was also not yet done; this was installed when the platform loops at Chatham were abolished for the platform lengthening. It was felt that another place for trains to overtake was needed. In the immediate post-war years the 4.15 pm Ramsgate-Victoria (SX) was booked 20 minutes at Chatham to enable the 'Kentish Belle' to overtake. Originally the latter train was named the 'Thanet Belle'; after a time it disappeared but a Pullman car ran in an ordinary service for a few years more.

The end of the war gradually saw station signs being replaced and lighting restored to its pre-war level, and some trains were put back to pre-war schedules. Summer Saturdays and Sundays, as I have already said, saw all types of locos and stock mustered when the crowds had their first holiday for many years. A number of stations still had the 'picture frame' type of station name signs behind glass with a wooden frame but most of these were replaced by the 'Southern green' sign with the target centre.

One Saturday afternoon we were indoors and we heard an enormous bang - almost like a bomb dropping. We were accustomed to the house shaking with fast trains going by and heavy shunting in the yard, but this was different, and on inspection we found that part of the front of the station was supported by a Maidstone and District bus that had collided with the canopy. This and the bus had to be taken away together. Later a small verandah was fitted over the station entrance. While ladders were erected at the front of the station a young lad was seen to climb up and was about to get into our upstairs window when we interrupted him!

In BR days, Bulleid 'West Country' 'Pacific' No 34013 *Okehampton* on the 12.45 Cannon Street-Ramsgate (Saturdays only) at Chatham in 1959 before the loop platforms were removed for platform lengthening. *Pamlin Prints*

4.
SHOREHAM-BY-SEA 1949-50
Trainee clerk

I was getting to the stage where I had to think about getting a job, and never having given it much thought I just assumed I would work on the railway. I think that nowadays young people are much more prepared for the change from school to work, which can be very shattering. I do not remember it being discussed at home or at school. Once again there was uncertainty at home as my father had been appointed to the post of station master at Worthing Central in 1949 but could not go as the previous occupant of the post had stayed on after his retirement date and, at that time, men were not being forced to take up their retirement at 65 years of age. My father had achieved an unlikely 'circuit' of the Southern Railway, having worked in all five divisions as they then were. The 'Southern' division of the SR was based at Southampton, Exeter was the headquarters of the 'Western' division of the 'Southern', and closer in was the 'London West' division with its offices at Woking. In the South East the headquarters of the 'London East' Division was at Orpington, and lastly was the 'London Central' Division sandwiched between with its head offices at Redhill.

I was particularly interested in timetables, and in my spare moments would help in my father's office by compiling simplifiers of the service for the signalmen. I could sit for hours pouring over timetables in the same way that someone else might be similarly occupied with looking at maps or books of reference and I felt that perhaps I could work in an enquiry office, if a vacancy arose.

In 1949 I took the clerical examination for British Railways (as it had then become) and immediately realised how unprepared I was for the outside world. There was a period of dictation from the Rule Book which boys without a railway background must have found rather strange. A period of the test dealt with general knowledge, and one of my questions was 'Where is Singapore?' Little did I then think that about 3 years later HM Government would send me out in khaki to find out! After the news that I had passed the examination, arrangements were made for me to take the clerical course at Clapham Junction. The 'Building' was a disused foot-bridge, and my problem was the noise from passing trains which made listening to the instructor particularly difficult, coupled with the fact that not only was one always more interested in which loco was hauling a particular train, but also there were two classes going on in the same room!

A mock-up ticket office was provided and each trainee had one or two sessions in the office with his colleagues as 'passengers' with the instructor seeing fair play and correcting the many mistakes. The tickets would be written out in pencil and used again next time! We had 'Monopoly' banknotes but real coins, so if any silver or copper was short at the end of the day the tea tin had to suffer. Otherwise it was made as realistic as possible. This course lasted about 9 weeks, and dealt with tickets, seasons, parcels and goods charging and accountancy. I found all this very bewildering - I had gone there thinking that I knew it all, but came away thinking I knew very little. Upon arrival each student was given an enormous page of figures to cross cast; I think they tried to break everyone's heart on the first day. I am not sure whether anyone really completed it or just hoped no one would notice it was wrong! People often say 'Well, I suppose all you have to know is how to issue a ticket', to which I reply 'There is that, as well as all the rest of the work'. The job is continually changing and so much of what one learns is of no further use after a short while. The accountancy was especially complicated and at one time I felt I would definitely fail, which fortunately I did not.

Some students came from as far distant as Salisbury, so were permitted to leave early to get home in reasonable time. I travelled up and down daily and learned much railway geography by looking at the indicators at stations and listening to the announcements, little thinking that one day I would be doing that job. Most of the announcements I could sort out, but the one that really baffled me was for trains going to 'Brom it off', which I subsequently found out was Bromley North!

Another amusing incident which comes to mind was when our train stopped at a signal at St Johns station one evening. Those who know this station will be aware that, as it has an island platform (and used to have two) the platform face is on the 'off side'. As we stopped, to our horror a man opened a door on the wrong side. On seeing this, everyone alighted on to the platform to allow him to get out, the train being very full - only to find that the reason he had opened the door was that his coat was caught in it!

As my father was now in lodgings in Worthing, it was decided that I would join him and ask for a posting to a London Central Division station. It had been the practice in the past for the railways to provide a station house for their station masters but the one at Worthing had been let to other staff some years before and the retiring SM had his own house. My father persuaded BR to buy a house for the SM but this of course took time; eventually a terraced house about 10 to 15 years old and about a mile from the station was bought. I shall never forget moving from a rambling station house to an ordinary residence with small rooms.

My grandparents were living with us by now and their room was going to be the front room downstairs - a bed, a chest of drawers, a wardrobe, various chairs and tables and all the usual accessories made it look like an auctioneer's sale room, not leaving room to move. This was indeed a great change for us. For one thing we had never had neighbours before, we were not used to having to allow time to get to the station, and we found it very quiet. Things went wrong from the moment we arrived as no electricity was available and we were forced to unpack our belongings by candlelight.

Having electric power in the house was something of a novelty. As we all loved our early morning cup of tea my mother was overjoyed to find a power point upstairs on the landing to make this possible, so the electric kettle was plugged in there overnight. We did not, however, notice when it was boiling and, after boiling dry, it burned through the floor boards and was found resting on the living room ceiling. We were lucky to escape a house fire - we must also have been very sound sleepers! (The kettle in question was not fitted with any type of switch and neither was the power point, or it would not have happened.)

There were disadvantages in living so far away from the station. We had a telephone installed but if my father were suddenly called out for an emergency, it took time to get to the station. I awoke one night to hear him on the telephone for a very long time. Apparently a theatrical company had obtained our number from the Police and had rung up in the night to say that their effects were in the Left Luggage office at the station and they wanted someone to unlock the office and give them their bags!

A free cinema ticket was available at certain stations in return for advertising and one evening we all made use of it. However, there was a deathly silence in the theatre and the manager walked to the front and asked the station master to come to his office as the station wanted him. It was his 'on call' night and he had left the theatre telephone number at the station, hence the announcement. (The 'on call' arrangement was with the adjacent SM, sometimes for alternate nights

DESCRIPTION.	COLOUR.	OVER-PRINT	AVAILABILITY.
Cheap Day.	1st white 3rd green.	CD or SC in red on return half.	one day i.e. day of issue.
Excursion.	1st yellow 3rd buff	Day - X on return half; half day - V in red on return half.	by trains as authorized
Daily Workmen.	Slate.	W. in red on return half	Day of issue.

3rd class standard single + 1/3 rounded up if nec. to next multiple of 3d. increased by R.R.

If a 1st class ticket is req.d then add 50% round up if nec. to next penny.

• Each stn. has its own list of cheap day tickets, fares are shown on each list & are usually on the basis of single fare for the return journey. NOT available for break of journey unless specially authorized.

• Stations affected are advised of each excursion & a supply of posters & handbills are provided giving full particulars. These should be prominently displayed. Not available for break of journey.

Each station has its own list of stns. to which these tickets are issued. The list gives exact fares to be charged. Tickets are issued by all trains which will enable holder to arrive at destination stn. on or

Pages from the author's note book of clerical instruction in 1949. Little of this applies today - in fact, some items had been amended even before the course had finished.

An up train entering Worthing Central, as it was then called, presumably in the 1930s as the conductor rail is laid, but the carriages look distinctly antique! ***Lens of Sutton***

or sometimes alternate weeks; the arrangement varied from one division to another).

Soon after joining BR, I was asked to go up to the Divisional Offices at Redhill and was offered a post in the 'Staff' Office. After some deliberation at home I rejected the opportunity; although everyone told me that I would be promoted far more quickly in such a post, I felt that I had always wanted to work on a station and head office routine work was not my 'cup of tea'. So, as vacancies were then few and far between, I was sent to Shoreham-by-Sea as a trainee. I found this very strange as my knowledge of the area was very poor, I knew no one and was very unsettled, having once again left my friends. Along the South Coast there was a very large number of retired people and I used to say, with a fair degree of accuracy, that I was the youngest person in the road!

An unidentified 0-6-0 hauling a freight past Shoreham-by-Sea. Note the short platforms, gas lamp and empty goods yard. ***Lens of Sutton***

6PUL unit No 3005 near Haywards Heath. These usually ran with a 6PAN, but with no gangway between the units. The compartments had no partitions above luggage rack level so one could overhear one's neighbour's conversations. ***John Scrase***

I never ceased to wonder how some of the passengers from the Worthing area afforded a First Class season to London and paid a Pullman supplement daily and bought breakfast on the train. (The London service was almost entirely made up of 6PUL and 6PAN stock, the Littlehampton and Portsmouth services were comprised of 2BILs, whilst the West Worthing service - known locally as the 'Short' - was 2NOL).

As I have mentioned before, my family were great walkers and every Sunday we would go for several miles. One summer Sunday my father had some business to attend to at West Worthing so we decided to take the train from Worthing Central and walk back. As we went through the barrier we saw that a train was in the platform so jumped in, only to find that it ran through West Worthing and the next three stations; then we realised that we were not in a 2NOL but in a SUB which was a return excursion to the suburban area via Arundel, and which stopped at Ford to reverse. We made a quick exit and came home hopefully unseen, but without our evening walk!

My training at Shoreham-by-Sea lasted several months. There were two ticket offices there. The 'up' office was a very small wooden affair and issued tickets 'up the line' and also seasons. The 'Red line' seasons were still in force which afforded passengers from certain South Coast resorts a cheaper season which was not valid at intermediate stations. This facility literally 'died out' when the holder ceased to travel. It surprised me how many passengers travelled by train to the next station only, the stations being very close on this line, and also how late in the evening people went out and still returned the same night! Of course Brighton is an all-the-year-round resort, so there is entertainment of all types to be found there.

It also seemed to me that passengers were less inclined to wait 10 minutes for a train where there was a frequent service than when the frequency was hourly or two-hourly, when they accepted it without complaint. One of the clerks in the 'up' office would always tell passengers that the next train was 'due now' (possibly because he did not know the service) - but it was usually almost true.

I thought it odd that the two clerks, one on either turn, were of different grades, but this practice has returned in recent years. One of the clerk's tasks was to count the bridge tolls which were brought in from the Old Shoreham toll bridge where the A27 crossed the Steyning line. This was a very busy road and the bridge was in poor condition and very narrow, so there was little chance of motorists rushing over without paying. A large volume of change was paid into the booking office once or twice a day.

The 'down' office issued tickets for journeys 'down' via Lancing, and also towards Horsham via Steyning (which was known as 'up'!). All parcel items in the widest sense of the word were also dealt with there. A GPO (or 'National') telephone was situated there, so that and parcels 'sheeting' (entering parcels for delivery on the carman's sheet) probably took up more time than issuing tickets. Office security was non-existent, the clerk having to go in and out constantly to the parcels counter. The parcels office would be stacked high each day with parcels for delivery to shops, etc, and different piles for various rounds. When the carman arrived the office door would be open for long periods whilst he loaded up. A very cold arrangement in the winter! We received far more items than we sent away, but quite a varied assortment of goods were charged up, stamped and despatched.

A tale was told of a cat being sent away in a basket. Apparently when it reached Brighton a member of the staff lifted the lid to speak to the occupant, who unfortunately felt that was the time to take his departure and ran down the road and over the nearest fence. Not to be beaten, the porter concerned picked up the buffet cat and slipped it into the basket instead, and no one was any the wiser. I could never vouch for the authenticity of that story!

In the evenings the clerk would be required to charge up the Worthing and District Growers Association market produce which was sent daily from local stations to London markets. This was loaded direct into vans so the clerk did not see the traffic but charged it up from the consignment notes. The Growers Association roughly covered an area along the coast from Portslade to Chichester, up the Steyning line and the 'Mid Sussex' line, and offered cheaper rates for produce, payment being made in bulk to BR from time to time. The traffic greatly decreased over the years due to increase in lorry traffic, which was prepared to carry the goods cheaper, demolition of nurseries for building, and various strikes and threats of strikes over the years. These items were parcels-rated traffic as were, strangely enough, livestock in vehicles attached to passenger trains. In the electrified area, of course, this was not possible, but occasionally a truck of livestock would be attached to a parcels train or a Steyning line service.

An elderly man came in one day and asked if he could sign for a horse which he was expecting. We sent a porter down to the yard to collect the wagon label and the waybill to see if any charges were due. After much delay the porter eventually produced the label and I entered the item in the 'Inwards Counter Book' for his signature, only to be told by the consignee that he could not read or write anyway!

Lancing College is situated behind Shoreham airport and the college luggage was dealt with at Shoreham-by-Sea when the students were breaking up or returning after a vacation. In the former instance, a list would be sent to the station and 'Luggage in Advance' labels prepared between times; on the day in question several lorry-loads of trunks, etc, would arrive and we would work overtime and try and put the labels on the right ones. There were always a few trunks which were not on the list, or labels for some which did not appear.

The practice for documenting ordinary parcels was simple. Unless the sender had a special arrangement with BR the clerk would pull off parcels stamps for the required amount and paste them to the parcel. A roll of stamps was supplied for almost any denomination from 1d to £1; they were consecutively numbered and had to be 'booked up' daily so that the value of stamps used could be worked out.

The train service at Shoreham-by-Sea was very frequent (about six trains each way each hour) and one ticket collector had to look after both sides; he spent most of his time running across the line, but rarely missed attending a train. All the trains were melodiously called out by the staff, while finger boards gave purely the destination. An old lady looked out of the train one day and asked 'Littlehampton?' We replied that it was, meaning the destination of the train, only the see her alight, thinking she had arrived!

Passengers often make the mistake of asking 'Where is this train going?' instead of 'Is it going to so and so?', as often the final destination tells them little. I was standing on the platform one day and a passenger said 'Am I on the right side for the Not London train?' I could not resist answering 'That's right. All stations to Not London'.

At about this time the 44-hour week for conciliation staff and 42-hour week for clerical grades were introduced and we saw a break from tradition where booking offices were closing at 8.30 or 9.00 pm (very early for those days) and 'rest day' working was introduced for 'wages grade' staff. It always seemed rather unfair that some staff should be rostered rest days and others booked to do less hours each day but get no rostered days off.

When anyone goes to live in an unfamiliar area it is inevitably difficult when answering the telephone to know who a firm or shop is and what they deal in. It is commonplace now for even young children to answer a telephone, but in those days householders with a telephone were in the minority, so I was understandably nervous of answering it, especially in view of the fact that I had to refer to someone else every time for the answer - not least on the occasion when I thought the caller said it was 'the BBC'. I knew this could not be so, and asked the clerk over me to take the call. It transpired that it *was* the BBC after all; they had a booster station nearby and were enquiring about the arrival of a parcel.

The chief clerk was a very small man and, as the railway telephone was fitted to the wall, it was necessary for him to climb up to answer it. He stood with one leg on the rung of the desk and the other on the skirting board; looking heavenward and shouting he just about made himself heard if the conversation was not too lengthy.

The public could also hand in a telegram form which was accounted for by counting the words and the amount paid into the traffic cash. The telegrams were sometimes sent by a day-tripper to a neighbour and the message would be something like 'Forgot to put out cat' or 'Left oven on', etc. Some of the local fishmongers who received fish off the early morning trains would hand in a telegram ordering their needs from Hull or Grimsby for the following morning. We found these rather a bind as the early mornings were very busy with incoming parcels to be entered on the carman's delivery sheet in addition to booking workmen's tickets, and the last thing we wanted at that time of the morning was extra work!

The railways had their own code book for telegrams concerned with railway business which were dictated over the telephone to the exchange or by the operator to us in the event of an incoming telegram. In the case of railway 'pass' telegrams we would use them to apply for a seat reservation for a passenger or perhaps to make enquiries for a parcel which had not arrived. A common trick to play on a new clerk was to hand him the telephone when a railway telegram was being dictated by the operator. The exchange would usually say 'I have a railway telegram for you', so the experienced clerk would say to the trainee 'Take this call, please, as I am a bit busy'. The poor trainee would be totally baffled as the words made no sense in themselves and he would think that he was listening to a foreign language.

Talking of missing parcels reminds me of a passenger who came in one day to complain of a suitcase being received but with the label missing. I hated dealing with 'missing and tracing' at any time, but this seemed a little out of the ordinary. We pointed out to the complainant how lucky he was to receive his case if the label was torn off, but he said that the label cost him 5 shillings about 25 years before and he didn't want to lose it. We agreed that it was a pretty dear item and no doubt he had had his value from it over the years, but he insisted on writing a letter of complaint. He asked us for some paper on which to write but we pointed out that one does not write a letter of complaint to a firm on their own notepaper, whereupon he pulled off a cheap ticket bill and wrote with a red crayon stating his main grounds of complaint. I sent the said excursion bill to the Divisional Office at Croydon (where it then was). I expect they had a chuckle!

It was a rare occurrence for clerks to write letters to the public as most correspondence would be done by the station master, who might have a typewriter of his own; but the clerk sometimes had to reply to a claim for

44

Medical Examination *(Continued)*

UTOPIA	Following ready to resume duty. Advise when and where he is to attend for medical examination.
DRAB	........may resume duty if his own doctor gives him a certificate to the effect that he is fit to do so.

MEETING

LIFFEY	Arrange..................meet me on arrival of following train.
RODENT	Meet the undermentioned by train named.
MEDOC	Arrange to be at my office at.............
SATURN	Wire when and where following will be held.
WELLAND	Arrange for the following person/s to attend at ....
NOCTURN	Arrange representative to attend at undermentioned place in regard to.............

MISCELLANEOUS

See Pages 65–67

MISSING AND TRACING

RHONE	Have you received the following? Wire reply.
PIKE	Following missing. Have you any trace? If so, send to.............
ELFANT	Can you trace receiving the following on or about the date given? If so, say how disposed of.
FALCON	No trace of receiving the following.
NILE	Following not to hand.
HUDSON	Following since to hand.
CORMOR	Your enquiry respecting the following not being to hand. Forwarded from here as under. I trace; wire me immediately received.
SERVIA	Certainly sent you; have further search made, and wire result.
DATUM	The undermentioned not received. Wire date and train sent.

45

Missing and Tracing *(Continued)*

Following not received. Say if any trace passing your station, and how disposed of, or trace forward.	GORIL
Not received. Same remark from transfer station. Trace forward.	HARRIER
Wire full particulars of forwarding following, giving date, reference to invoice, etc.	LILAC
Wire time and date and where following were handed to.............	ALBANY
Let me know how you disposed of the following, or if still on hand.	SPINACH
No trace of forwarding the following.	FUNGUS
Following said to have been sent you on or about undermentioned date by station named. Wire particulars of receipt and proof of delivery if effected.	FOX
Following sent you in wagon named, said not to hand at destination. Say how disposed of by you and trace forward.	JIRAF
Following missing, urgently wanted. Have special enquiries made and if with you forward immediately and reply.	CHIK
Following missing from train named, said last seen at your station. Send to.............	RUDD
Following, which left undermentioned station on date named, is urgently wanted. If with you, forward to............. Reply.	WOLF
Following on hand at station named without address. Wire if you can trace passing, or if wanted by you.	QUAIL
Following not wanted here.	ERMIN
Following invoiced from you not to hand. Wire date, train, truck, and to what point sent, and trace forward.	CYGNET

Some of the code words for use in railway telegrams - quite a mystery to those not 'in the know'.

damage relating to parcels or goods traffic, and it was usually done in pencil in order to get a good carbon copy (pen and ink were seldom hard enough to achieve this). What the recipient thought I cannot imagine, as the clerk concerned was not one of our best scribes. The address on the envelope from the claimant to us looked like a copy of the clerk's writing - obviously the recipient could not read the name and so copied it as best he could!

All sorts of items used to travel by train, many of which have since been lost to other forms of transport, but in the season it was commonplace to have pigeons offered for transit. Pigeon fanciers would put their birds on training flights by sending them further and further away from home and timing their flight. Some would be sent to a station to be released; station staff would take the basket to an overbridge, open it, release the birds, noting the time of release, and return the basket to the senders. More than once birds were released only to find that they were not for release at all - the consignee was very put out to say the least! It was at another local station that a porter complained to us that, when he released the pigeons, they would not go away. When we enquired where he had liberated them, he said 'In the staff room'. The birds were making themselves at home on the lockers and shelves, and brooms and brushes had to be brought into use to move them on.

5.
SOUTHWICK AND SINGAPORE 1950-54
From booking office to barracks

I was beginning to feel that it was time for me to take over an office alone. The period of training seemed to vary according to when a vacancy occurred somewhere - nowadays the reverse is the case, where an applicant is taken on with a vacancy in view.

Eventually out of the blue a clerk at Southwick, the next station towards Brighton, resigned, so I was earmarked to take over the position. The clerk on the other shift was very pleasant and we got on very well together. There were just two turns, early and late, but the Sunday turn was a 'split' turn, about 9.00 am to 12 noon and 4.00 pm to 9.00 pm, if I remember rightly. But naturally the whole day was wasted.

London Brighton & South Coast Railway.

Partridge Green to

Southwick

The middle of the day was covered by the platform staff in the office but, as the office was so far from the platform, they could not deal with both, but this part of the day was deemed to be the quietest. The platform staff had to be forgiven for making mistakes as they had no training whatsoever - it was purely a cheap way of covering the hours. We made a cash balance on each turn by recording the next number to issue of each tube of tickets and balancing our parcels accountancy books (13 altogether) daily in addition to many daily, weekly and monthly returns. Railway accountancy bears no resemblance to that undertaken by an outside firm for obvious reasons. One of our weekly returns required a reason for an increase or decrease in revenue when compared to the corresponding week of the previous year. Few reasons were logical except, for example, that it was Easter last year. If a large increase was shown one week, a favourite reason was 'new building in the area' but, of course, this did not apply in reverse!

The office at Southwick was a great barn of a place and very cold in the winter. It was gas lit which gave a little heat, and running water was put in later, during the time that I was there. The platform staff had to be cajoled into lighting a fire, and often the wood and coal came from the track, so were very wet. (With locos going by coal often fell off the tenders, but it was not very suitable for open fires.) I was amazed to find the fire going magnificently one winter's morning and did not understand how the Leading Porter had had such success until I opened the table drawer to take out some labels and found the bottom of the drawer only about a foot square and labels all over the floor. It was obvious where the rest of the drawer had gone.

The leading porter on my shift was a most likeable fellow but very accident prone. One day he brought a box of chickens off a train down to the office but, as the base was made only of cardboard, it fell out and I was surrounded by fighting hens with all the accompanying mess, and the owner had the task of

The front of Southwick station in LB&SCR days. The frontage and signal box had changed little for many years, but the trees and the gun were not evident in immediate post-war years. *Lens of Sutton*

rounding them up! On another occasion he was bringing a box of cake and a can of disinfectant to the office. He tripped and the result can be anticipated. All the cake had to be destroyed.

From time to time he would borrow a theatre ticket from a local shopkeeper who had a free pass as he exhibited advertisements for cinemas, etc, in his window. I accompanied him on one or two occasions but usually something went wrong. If he remembered his spectacles he would forget the tickets or vice versa, but he had a heart of gold and would never do anyone a bad turn. It was several years later that he had a most dreadful accident when he was badly burned by the conductor rail after bending down to attend to brakes on a van train and allowing his hand lamp to come into contact with the electric current; he was away from work for many months.

Most of the ticket offices left a lot to be desired as regards safety in those days. Somehow, although being constantly warned, clerks seldom locked the office door and all and sundry found their way in. This was partly because the handling of parcels traffic meant that both staff and public had to have access to the office as the ticket and parcels office were combined.

The office at Southwick was then at the bottom of the subway slope and quite a way from the platform - the only way of calling assistance was by use of a bell which worked spasmodically. I don't think I shall ever forget suddenly seeing a very drunk West African standing beside me one evening eyeing the till. He was very tall and extremely broad - at least he appeared so to me then. I do not know how long he stayed but it seemed an eternity - he had left a kitbag in the Left Luggage and he wanted some items from it. When he ordered me to take them out, which I did, he then asked why I was interfering with his things! I was absolutely terrified, but felt that someone was watching over me when he suddenly went as quickly as he had arrived and took nothing.

In any dangerous or hairy circumstance one can usually find something to laugh about and, like most jobs, we would recount our adventures to others, and retired staff would do likewise. An elderly man had been a clerk at the same office and he told me about an instance when he too wished the door had been locked. The office had a large loft and we had explored this as, no doubt, others had done before. My pensioner friend recounted how he had once explored it and, whilst up there, the station master had come into the office. Finding it apparently empty, he stood in the doorway facing outwards in order to wait for the clerk's return. Behind his back the clerk slipped down from the attic and carried on his work. The station master eventually caught sight of him and asked him where he had been, whereupon the clerk replied 'Where have I been? Had I been out and returned you would have seen me'. He said the SM never knew where the man had been and just assumed that the clerk had been there all the time and he must have suffered a mental blackout.

Southwick was not busy, but even the quietest place has its moments, and of course passengers were inclined to arrive in bunches (for instance from buses) and it was always hard to convince callers who had telephoned and had to wait for a reply that one was busy. It is fatal to lift the receiver and ask a caller to wait, as one can so easily forget about the call and find the receiver still off the hook a while later. The telephone at Southwick would be a collector's piece nowadays. It was of the upright design and the earpiece was separate and hung on a rest at the side.

I well remember a lady at that station complaining bitterly about a small matter and finishing by asking 'Do you know who I am?' Of course, I said that I did not. I think she was even more livid when she explained that her husband was a Brighton and Hove Albion player, but the name meant nothing to me and she probably noticed my ignorance of football. It was rather a different 'kettle of fish' when I had the pleasure, a few years later, of handing over a parcel to Sir Jack Hobbs. My knowledge of cricket greatly exceeded that of football.

The types of tickets held at Southwick were many and varied. There were workmen's tickets to certain destinations, day, weekend, and overnight tickets for commercial travellers (they also enjoyed a cheap left luggage facility for 3d an item), and a discount of about five-sevenths for forces and members of the merchant service of which quite a few used Southwick after leaving their ships in Shoreham harbour. There was a facility called 'bulk travel' for passengers with free travel warrants, day, half-day and evening excursions, cheap fares for anglers ('with rod and line' being the requirement). These passengers usually went to the most remote station on a river and most wanted connections looked up in the timetable, which was quite an education.

We also issued a large number of privilege tickets there, as Lancing and Brighton railway works were nearby and employed a large workforce. Each person had to hand in a form for every 'priv' ticket issued. (Each working day a steam train ran from Brighton to Lancing Works with staff. Special very old coaches were used and hauled by one or two tank engines - it was always known as the 'Lancing Belle'). The most unlikely ticket which we held at Southwick was a blank card marked 'Shipwrecked mariner'. Sadly I never issued one but I often visualised a bedraggled seaman with torn, very wet trousers stepping out of the sea with his belongings in a handkerchief demanding the facility. In a dark corner of the cupboard we found a bundle of tickets to Shoreham Airport which had closed a few years before and, being too honest, we returned them to the Audit Department.

The Audit Department would check all collected season tickets very thoroughly and, if charged wrongly, would issue a debit or credit schedule which would be a suspended (or outstanding) item and had a considerable nuisance value; if we undercharged a passenger we were expected to call on him and collect the balance due, often months later. You can imagine the response which a lad of 16 got, not in uniform, knocking on a door in the evening without even a letter of authority.

My station never had a through train to London on a regular basis and only a few Portsmouth trains stopped there. A few in the evening peak called when the service did not conform with the regular-interval service and for some reason the 1.16 pm Brighton-Portsmouth also called (if the driver remembered). We had an occasional Horsham train but most of the day the service comprised of West Worthing or Littlehampton trains to and from Brighton. I would spend many

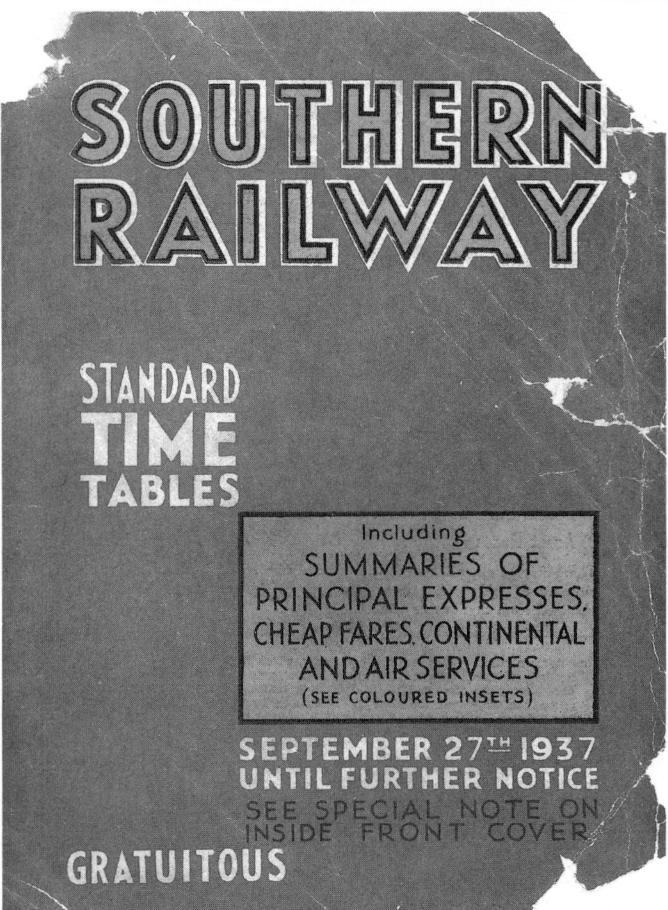

A railway 'antique' found behind a ticket rack at Southwick - the cover and map from a Southern Railway timetable dating from 1937.

hours in the signal box which was very small and had only two stop and two distant signals; with only short sections between Shoreham West, Shoreham East, Kingston Wharf and Southwick, then a slightly longer section to Portslade, there was almost always a train 'on the block'. The signalling was standard three-position block and trains were constantly having to be stopped in the up platform to await clearance. For this reason some stops were included in the timetable as the services in question would never get a clear run anyway. One of these was a train from Horsham to Brighton which was booked to call at Southwick but not Portslade, the only one so to do.

I was aware that sooner or later I would be called up for National Service and had mixed feelings about it. I suppose everyone has some fear of the unknown but the possibility of travel and adventure appealed. I liked Southwick but felt sure that I would not come back there. ('It was only a boy's job.') I was getting used to leaving friends almost as soon as I had made them but I realised that I would catch up with them again upon return, and agreed to write to some of them. The Royal Engineers seemed a good idea; I had relatives in the corps and had a vague idea that I would like to get to Longmoor (the Royal Engineers' Railway Centre). We were given long talks about being put into the most useful postings; we could state our options but this counted for little. There was only one recruit who got a 'home' posting and he was a 'regular' (ie not a national serviceman).

When the day eventually came I was post-

My instructions to report to the Royal Engineers at Aldershot. The journey was made via Havant and Guildford.

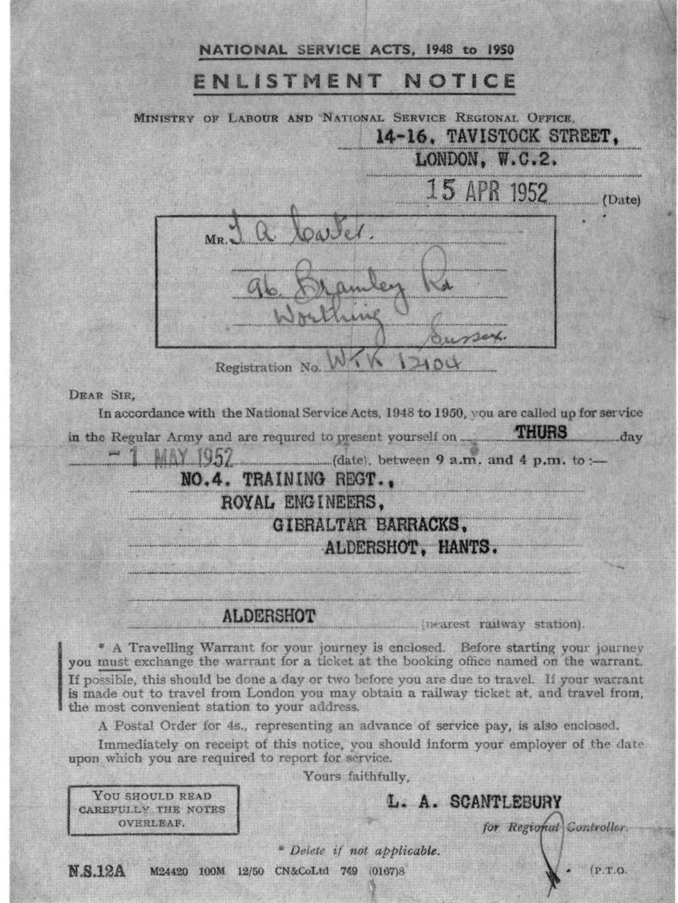

NATIONAL SERVICE ACTS, 1948 to 1950

ENLISTMENT NOTICE

MINISTRY OF LABOUR AND NATIONAL SERVICE REGIONAL OFFICE,
14-16, TAVISTOCK STREET,
LONDON, W.C.2.
15 APR 1952 (Date)

MR. J. A. Carter.
96. Bramley Rd
Worthing
Sussex.

Registration No. WTK 12104

DEAR SIR,

In accordance with the National Service Acts, 1948 to 1950, you are called up for service in the Regular Army and are required to present yourself on THURS day - 1 MAY 1952 (date), between 9 a.m. and 4 p.m. to :—

NO.4. TRAINING REGT.,
ROYAL ENGINEERS,
GIBRALTAR BARRACKS,
ALDERSHOT, HANTS.

ALDERSHOT (nearest railway station).

* A Travelling Warrant for your journey is enclosed. Before starting your journey you must exchange the warrant for a ticket at the booking office named on the warrant. If possible, this should be done a day or two before you are due to travel. If your warrant is made out to travel from London you may obtain a railway ticket at, and travel from, the most convenient station to your address.

A Postal Order for 4s., representing an advance of service pay, is also enclosed.

Immediately on receipt of this notice, you should inform your employer of the date upon which you are required to report for service.

Yours faithfully,

L. A. SCANTLEBURY
for Regional Controller.

YOU SHOULD READ CAREFULLY THE NOTES OVERLEAF.

* Delete if not applicable.

N.S.12A M24420 100M 12/50 CN&CoLtd 749 (0167)8 (P.T.O.

ed to Malta Barracks at Aldershot and, after six weeks, was sent to Elgin. We had a special train which ran up the East Coast route. It seemed an awful long way away and even in August was very cold.

I will not bore you with the remainder of my army career excepting the parts which involved me with railways. After about three months, my next posting was to Long Marston, an enormous depot with lengthy rail sidings situated in three counties, Warwickshire, Worcestershire and Gloucestershire, on a branch line from Stratford upon Avon to Honeybourne. Although I did not then know that part of the country, I felt as though I was almost at home after the North of Scotland and intended going home as often as possible.

There was only a handful of us transferred from Elgin and we travelled down through Aviemore and Stirling, passing some of the loveliest scenery in the British Isles, but not really taking in the full pleasure of it. We continued on to Birmingham and here I made a mistake which someone more conversant with the area would not have made. Upon arrival at New Street I enquired of a taxi driver how far away Snow Hill station was and was told it was a long way. He drove us for miles through back streets and, upon arrival, we met up with the others who had walked the few hundred yards.

I became quite fond of the lines around Stratford, perhaps feeling 'at home' with small country stations, some unstaffed, some oil-lit and served by ex-GWR railcars. In those days every station was different, their signal boxes, buildings and lights all being distinctive - now so much has been standardised, destroying character.

After completing a storeman's course at Long Marston, we knew that we were earmarked for an overseas posting and we were playing the waiting game. Although we had had our passes withdrawn, some of the lads were taking chances and going home at weekends. We told the regimental police on the gate that we were going into Honeybourne (which was permitted without a pass). Anyone knew that to be untrue, but I suppose the onus was on us. I made up my mind I would take a chance of going home to Worthing for a '48' (service jargon for 48 hours leave). All went well until my return on Sunday evening. It was a very cold, foggy December evening the likes of which we rarely see now, thankfully. On arrival at Paddington there were no relevant trains on the indicator. I knew that there would be trouble if I did not get back by midnight as I would be missed. As the service was so disrupted I looked for a train going anywhere in the right direction.

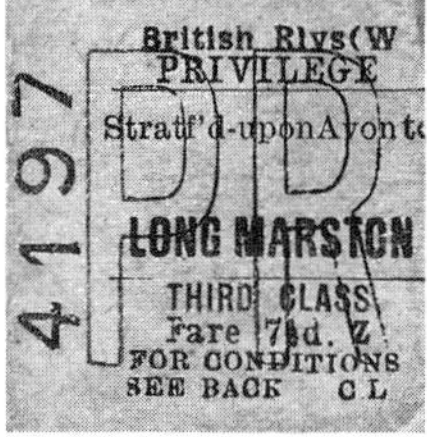

One of my 'privs' between Stratford upon Avon and Long Marston, dated November 1952.

At long last a service for Leamington Spa was indicated and I took it gladly. After much delay in the fog we eventually arrived, quite prepared to take a taxi back to camp, but Military Police were checking passes at the ticket barrier, and our hearts sank. Gradually we moved further and further to the back of the queue, unsure what line to adopt. Eventually one of the MPs said to the other 'These blokes are all for Long Marston, put them in the truck', so no more passes were checked and we followed the others for a free lift back to the barracks. Once again my guardian angel was on duty! Needless to say I did not attempt any more leave as, with winter coming on, it was too risky as it would have meant a Court Martial if anyone had been found out. After a few days we were transferred to a transit camp at Malvern. After spending Christmas Day doing nothing there we eventually went by special train to Liverpool and sailed on 31 December 1952 on the troopship *Empire Pride*. That was nothing to be proud of - a ship with a less appropriate name I cannot imagine!

Much of my time in the Far East is another story, but all the while I was trying to get a job connected with railways. This seemed a false hope as although I was sent to a stores department in Singapore with siding access, only one man ran this side of things and it seemed a lost cause. He was responsible for ordering wagons, etc, and seeing the daily diesel-operated freight in and out of the depot. However, I got friendly with him and after a while I was appointed to help him; then, when he returned to England, I took over the job. The task was attractive in that although I had to start early and finish later than the others, I did no guards, PE or parades. An extra part of my work was checking in and out the lorries that brought manual workers, ensuring that the vehicles were all reasonably suitable for carrying civilians, checking their work notes and trying to keep the traffic orderly. Easier said than done!

My work did not take the whole day and sometimes I had next to nothing to do on the railway side, but I was responsible for despatching items by train, either ordering wagons if necessary or taking them to the local station for passenger train transit. If wagons were being received loaded or empty, a goods train would arrive and have to be shown into the yard and the wagons placed. The only way we knew when to expect the train was by a field telephone; this sometimes worked, and if it did either I was not there to answer it, or if someone else did they invariably forgot to tell me until it was too late, and we then saw the loco placing the trucks in totally the wrong position.

Whilst there I had a short holiday in Penang, although I had to travel up in uniform and 'guard' the train by standing on the open gangway with a loaded rifle between the coaches, an ideal target for a sniper. I would not have seen anyone in the jungle even in daylight.

Eventually my 'python' date (army jargon for date of return) came at Easter 1954 and I was on the list for return on the *Empire Trooper* bound for Southampton. I was ruing my misfortune as all the others that I knew were going home then were to go on the *Empire Windrush* and I was to be separated from them again. As it happened I was more than fortunate as the latter was the troopship which caught fire and sank in the Mediterranean. Most of the soldiers escaped but lost all their possessions.

After landing at Southampton and spending a few days at Barton Stacey near Andover it was demob date and back to Civvy Street. All those who had completed two years National Service had then to enlist for the Territorial Army for three years. Each year there were compulsory weekends away and a fortnight's camp each summer. One of the largest exercises ever undertaken in peacetime by the TA was held at Bulford on Salisbury Plain and I was one of those who went on the through train which ran specially. It started at Hastings and ran via Brighton, Havant, Chandlers Ford and Stockbridge. This was the one and only time I went on the Bulford branch; a special station for Bulford camp was beyond the public station.

Bulford station - the line continued on to Bulford Camp. The station was closed to passengers on 30 June 1952, but the line was used for troop trains after that date. *Real Photographs*

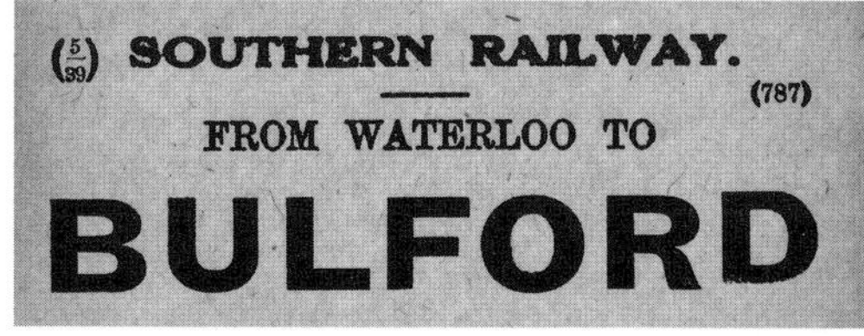

6.
BRIGHTON AND HOVE 1954-56
Enquiry and relief work

On my return from the services, I had a short leave and then reported back to BR at Worthing Central under my father. It was necessary for me to have a short 'refresher' as things were changing constantly. There was a bit of variety at Worthing for clerical staff, and it had a large staff establishment. Ticket offices were provided on both sides of the station and there were also clerks in the parcels office, enquiry office and in the station master's office (the latter clerk would do typing and arrange rosters and general correspondence). In addition to these positions, a clerk was provided by BR to staff the office near the pier together with a member of the Worthing Corporation staff who would give the public information about accommodation, etc.

Most clerks have at some time or other locked themselves out of the office, a situation that proves difficult to overcome as the doors are usually well constructed and difficult to force. One day a relief clerk working at the pier office did just that, and, as the Corporation clerk had gone home, he had to walk to the station without his jacket in search of a spare key. The station did not keep a spare key, so the next place to try was the Town Hall. He got there only to find it closed, so had to proceed by bus, still coatless, to the home of the appropriate officer for the spare key.

I knew my period at Worthing was only temporary. Whilst I enjoyed it, it was rather embarrassing at times if people did not know who the station master was, or rather who I was, and asked awkward questions.

After about two months I was informed that I was to be a 'summer hand' at Brighton enquiry office. I was interested in timetables, but continental enquiries and bookings were then very rare. The public telephone was in the same office, so each clerk would take a turn on the telephone. In fact, the operator did not bother to ring as, after finishing each call, we would lift the receiver again and take the next one!

A colleague had an unfortunate complaint directed at him one day when he was on telephone duty. A lady caller had asked for connections to a holiday resort and he gave her several. She asked him the arrival time, and he said 'Which one?' She said '6.1? Thank you. Goodbye'. Apparently she booked a taxi for 06.01 and was not pleased when she had a bill for a long wait from the taxi firm.

It was while we were there that we were plunged into a strike of drivers which lasted several weeks. Whilst it was unpleasant being at the receiving end of passengers' complaints and being able to tell them little, it had its lighter moments. A passenger came in and asked 'Can I get a connection back to Micheldever please?', to which the Scottish clerk replied 'I don't think that there is a station there'. The passenger replied 'There was

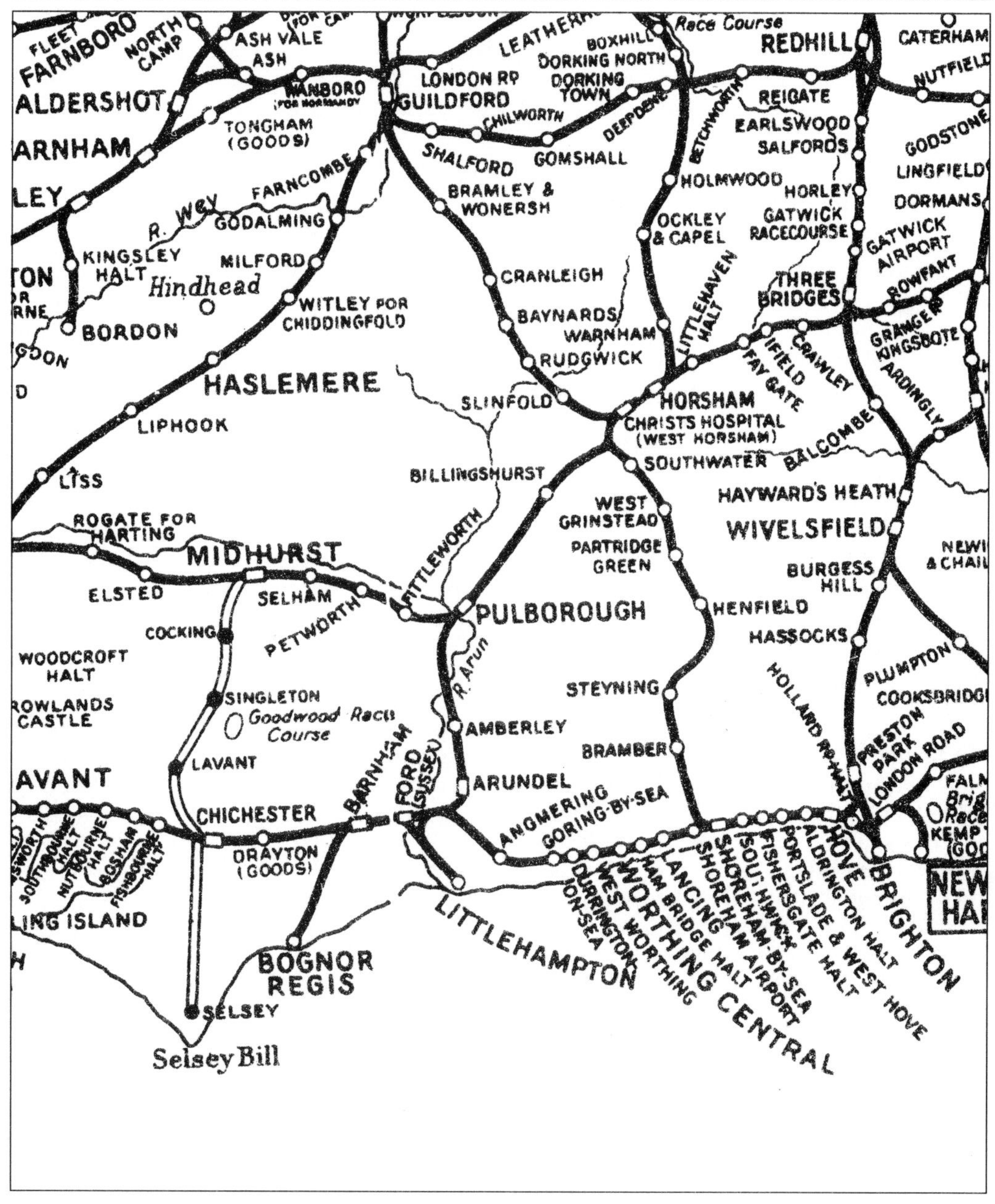

Lines around Shoreham, from a Southern Railway carriage map of the system. ***Author's Collection***

this morning when I left. I am the station master.'

Some passengers would come into the office and say that they had a car going to London if anyone would like a lift, and we were amused when a young lad whom we knew came in one morning and said 'I have a cycle going to London if anyone would like a lift'. Two elderly ladies followed him out before realising what he had said.

We were getting tired of not being in a position to tell the passengers anything, and to go on day after day like this began to wear us down. One of my colleagues got similarly fed up with giving the same negative news over and over again, so one day he waited until the office was full of eager passengers, then made the following stupendous announcement: 'I can't tell you nothing and that's all I can tell you.' Talk about an anti-climax!

A task which most of us had to undertake periodically was to visit the Corn Exchange where conferences were held and give rail information to delegates. I found this rather tedious since whilst the conference was in progress I had few customers, but at lunchtime and at the close of the day a handful of people would make timetable enquiries. If they wanted reservations I would take the details back to the station and bring the tickets the next day. Eventually an elderly relief clerk asked to change with me as he preferred the 'middle turn' without the rough and tumble of station life; this took away the boredom for me, and put me back at the station which I preferred.

Brighton also had a town office staffed by BR and I worked there on one or two occasions, but I always preferred the hustle and bustle of the station. Somehow it did not feel as though I was at work when walking through the town. It was at this office that a passenger bought and paid for an 'all systems' timetable. He tore the cover off, neatly folded that and the map into his pocket and threw the complete book into the bin. Perhaps that is what he thought of our service. We retrieved the timetable and used it, as our supply copies soon wore out and we were glad of extras.

I was always amazed to see that, whatever time of the morning I arrived at the station enquiry office, there would always be someone waiting. Holidaymakers would be at the station at 7 am for their seat reservation or whatever, saying 'When I am at work I get in the habit of rising early'. I think that is a habit I could easily shake off!

We would make reservations on the through steam trains to Bournemouth, Cardiff and Plymouth and also the numerous 'summer' trains to the Midlands. A passenger would be asked whether he preferred smoking or non-smoking accommodation and whether facing the engine or not. Most of these trains going north started at Hastings and, after reversing at Eastbourne, Brighton and Redhill, it appeared to matter not whether they had facing or back to engine seats as at some part of the journey someone would be satisfied. A through train to Birkenhead ran each weekday and joined up at Redhill with a portion from the Kent Coast. Redhill had a double junction but only three platforms, and with these trains loco-hauled it is not surprising that some suffered quite lengthy delays. The number of light engine moves alone must have been considerable.

Brighton also had steam services to Horsham via Steyning, to Tunbridge Wells, to East Grinstead, and to London via Oxted. These were not at regular timings and in some cases passengers would take the Hastings train to Lewes where the steam train started.

Motive power would sometimes be a 'Brighton Atlantic', 'H1' or 'H2' Class, on the 'Bournemouth', but latterly most of the westbound trains would be hauled by 'West Country' Class locos. The East Grinstead and Tunbridge Wells trains had a variety of motive power - 'Schools', 'West Countries' and Standard tanks, to name but a few.

On Summer Saturdays there were through trains to the Midlands and the North, but after a few years, when electrification took off in a big way, these dwindled as it was often quicker to go via London. (In recent years, with the growth of Gatwick Airport and cross-Channel traffic, these have reappeared using Kensington as an advertised stop.) Reservations were not always possible on these northbound trains, but when they were made they were not very successful as invariably the train ran in on a different platform at Brighton and the carriage labels faced the wrong side, so no one got their seats and it ended as a free-for-all. In most cases these trains were notoriously bad time-keepers. The 'Bournemouth' and the 'Plymouth' were the best, possibly as they were Southern throughout (until the boundaries changed).

Steam around Brighton

'E4' 0-6-2T No 32479 leaves Brighton with the 15.59 Horsham train on 8 September 1960. This train would have run via Steyning (see Chapter 8). *Jbhn Scrace*

'Brighton Atlantic' 4-4-2 No 32421 *South Foreland* at Brighton. *Real Photographs*

A through Plymouth-Brighton service at Havant behind 'Battle of Britain' No 34067 *Tangmere*. There were at that time only three trains in each direction daily using the curve from Havant to Cosham - the Brighton-Bournemouth, Brighton-Cardiff and Brighton-Plymouth. *Real Photographs*

Electric services around Brighton

2BIL unit No 2062 at Goring by Sea with the 14.30 Brighton-Littlehampton in 1971. *John Scrase*

HAL unit No 2627 with a Brighton service at Angmering, also in 1971. *John Scrase*

In addition to the London service there was one electric through train to Horsted Keynes each Monday to Friday via Haywards Heath. On the 'West' side there were regular electric trains to West Worthing, Littlehampton and Portsmouth and one or two direct to Bognor Regis.

When the summer was over it was intended that I should do temporary relief work, but there were so few vacancies that I was rarely called on. I based myself in the station master's office at Brighton and they were pleased to retain me for routine tasks, but as it continued week after week I became rather bored.

I was surprised to be sent to Streatham Common on one occasion, but that was an isolated occurrence and I was rarely called up to the London area again. I worked at Preston Park a couple of times, as that came under the jurisdiction of the Brighton SM, but still week after week I was mostly 'spare'. Football matches and race meetings often mean extra work for the railways, and I was asked to go to Lingfield to assist once or twice. The part I enjoyed most was the journey, and each time I travelled there or back I used a different route. The lines around East Grinstead were, to me, a new adventure.

I also spent a few days in Eastbourne enquiry office, and both there and at Lewes, where I relieved for a few days, the clerk operated the telephone switchboard. I found this very bewildering as nothing like that had ever come my way and I had had no training; but I suppose I did it right as no one complained. At Lewes the little switchboard was in the ticket office; the cords were not weighted and at the end of the turn I finished up with yards of tangled cable which had to be sorted out.

Going to other stations was a great education, as each was different in some way. Some passengers could be quite helpful, and when asking for their ticket would say 'Third row down, fourth from the left and you will

A picture from the *Worthing Gazette* recording the retirement of my father in 1956.

Exterior (1982) and platform (1971) views of Hove station. Note the 'LB&SCR' monogram in tiles at the left of the station entrance. *John Scrace*

find it difficult to get the ticket out as it frequently gets stuck'. Passengers also sometimes use local names for stations which the uninitiated may find strange. Many are based on old station names, for example Ham Bridge for East Worthing, and travellers often refer to Peckham Rye as Rye Lane, or Well Hall for Eltham.

The following summer saw me back in Brighton enquiry office, but I was dreading the winter if it meant 'kicking my heels' again. As it worked out I need not have worried as a reorganisation of staff at Hove meant a vacancy there. This was my first taste of a busy station as the season ticket issue was very high; there was also a fairly high volume of parcels traffic and left luggage. At that time Hove was one of the more modern offices, as glass-fronted offices were rare indeed.

Passengers could reserve seats on the up London trains and this involved marking off a chart rather like those used in theatres and sending it to Littlehampton, where the train would start, so that the seats could be labelled. As we did not get much call for this facility it was easy to forget to send the chart away, so the seat might easily be occupied by the time the train reached Hove. If one remembered in time, the best thing was to have a word with the Foreman who would shepherd the passenger to the nearest empty seat and say 'Oh, here's your reservation'! He probably put them in A27 when their ticket said D6, but if it was a smoker facing direction of travel who was worried?

At Hove an old office was provided on the north side of the station and was only used when Brighton and Hove Albion played at home. A clerk would go over with a few tickets to issue just until the football crowd had gone.

At both Brighton and Hove it was commonplace to see public figures and 'showbiz' personalities and most were very pleasant.

The duties at Hove were such that I had to work two weeks late turn out of three. Apart from the early turn there was a 1.00 pm start and a 3.30 pm turn, the chief clerk always doing the 'second early'. To do the Sunday turn meant either arriving by the first train a little late or coming by road. I decided to cycle in from Worthing one Sunday, but did not allow enough time; I cycled in just as the first train arrived, having got up much earlier and being very wet and tired into the bargain!

7.
SOUTHAMPTON 1956-59
Boat train traffic at the Terminus

I was very happy at Hove but was thinking of getting married and was hoping to rent a house in Southampton which had just come empty.

I had first to endeavour to get a transfer there, and eventually in 1956 I was informed that a vacancy at Southampton Terminus existed if I was interested. I wondered whether I was making a wise move as there was so much scope in the Brighton area and travelling was easy, whereas clerical posts around Southampton were few and far between except for the few large surrounding towns and in the Divisional Offices, and the steam service was not very frequent.

I found the 'terminus' a different world. After the rush and tear of Hove, I could not have found a greater contrast. Seasons issues were almost nil and if someone wanted one the other clerks would consult me! Issues of

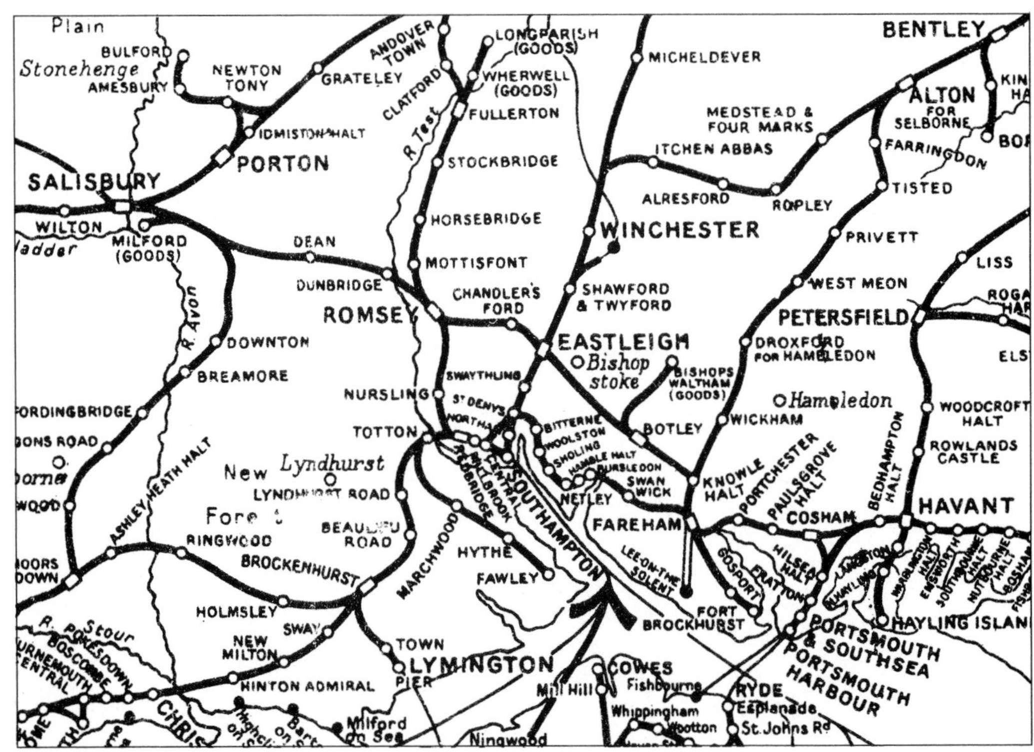

Lines around Southampton, from a Southern Railway carriage map of the system. *Author's Collection*

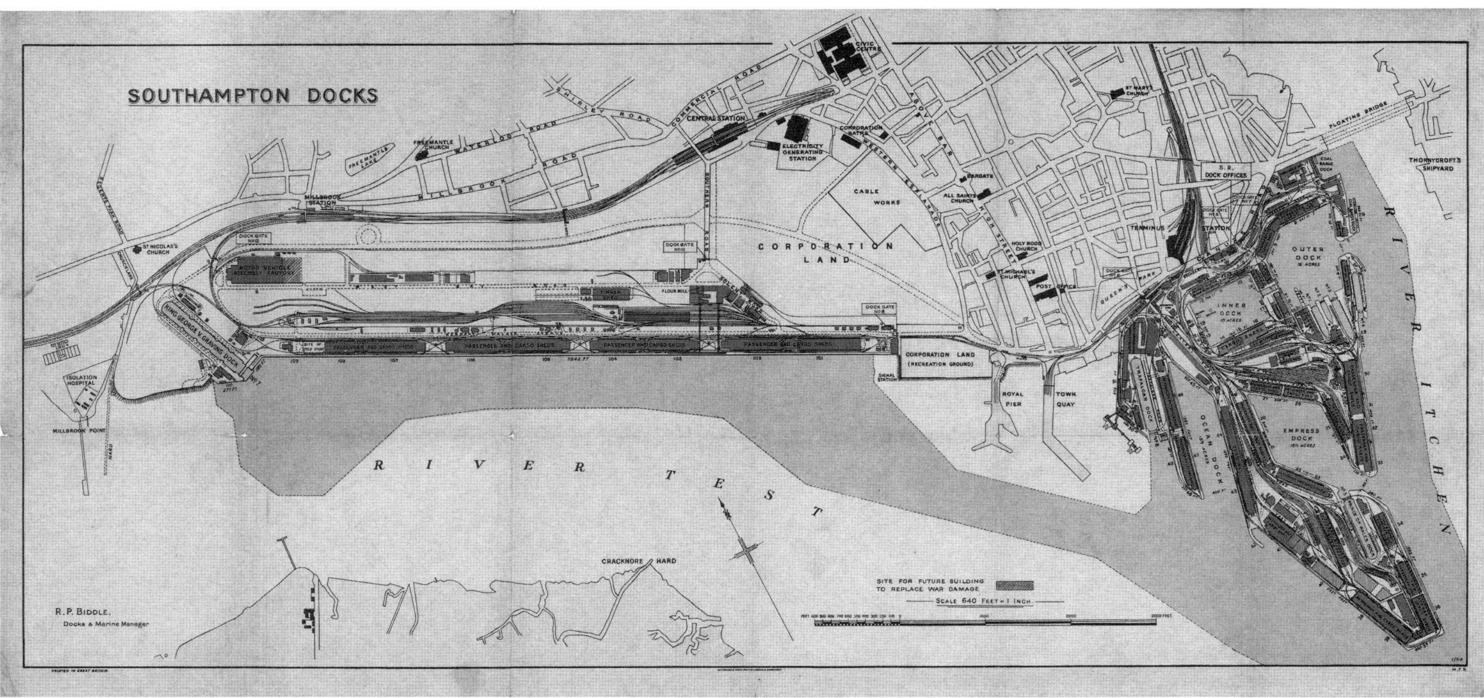

A 1954 map of Southampton Docks showing Terminus station on the right, with the Ocean Terminal building below it beside Ocean Dock, and Southampton Central in the top centre. Few of these buildings exist now. *Author's Collection*

ordinary tickets were also quite sparse and between trains we closed the office to go to the bank and empty pennies from the toilet locks. (It was the only station where we collected more money in the gents toilets than the ladies, as lady passengers were few and far between). There was no rush period whatever, and the time seemed long. Again I found the terminology strange. In different areas things are called by different names, so I had to learn the local names for things; for example, a sack barrow may be a pair of wheels or a blade depending where you are, whilst tips could be 'fluff' or 'weasels'. It was obvious that I was an alien.

At that time I did not take much notice which locos worked into the station, but I think that most trains were hauled by a 'T9' 4-4-0 or 'M7' 0-4-4, and a miscellany of old LSWR stock was used. Some WR locos also worked in and when *City of Truro* was brought back into service a certain amount of interest was provoked. Our service was very odd. There was a through train to Waterloo at 6.00 am and after that we ran a hotchpotch of trains to an assortment of destinations such as Alton, Reading, Bournemouth, Fawley, Didcot (via Winchester Chesil), Cheltenham via Stockbridge, and a few locals to Eastleigh or Winchester City.

Late at night the up and down mail trains met at the Terminus side by side and letter mail was exchanged there in large volume. The night down 'Weymouth' did not call at Southampton Central and the station inspector would walk through the train to waken any sleeping passengers and point out that Brockenhurst was the next stop, but about once a week someone would write in and claim a taxi fare as they were not told that it did not stop at the Central!

When the Hampshire diesel-electric multi-

'The Old Lady of Terminus Terrace'. ***Southern Evening Echo***

One of the initially unpopular Hampshire DEMUs, unit No 1102, near Millbrook in 1978. *John Scrase*

ple units first appeared they were very unpopular. For one thing the seating capacity was much reduced and generally speaking the trains were much shorter than the 'steamers'; there was also a lot of correspondence in the local press about the noise from the diesels, although this was later reduced.

Old residents in the city still called the Terminus the 'Docks' station, and some confusion came about because, on a Sunday morning, the Channel Islands boat train was advertised in the public timetable from Southampton Docks to Waterloo. Passengers came to the Terminus to purchase a ticket and then had to be directed to the Channel Islands berth in the 'Old Docks', that is assuming that they had allowed enough time.

There was quite a large payroll at the Terminus with cleaners, shunters, parcels staff, signalmen at four boxes (Southampton Yard, Northam Junction, Chapel Crossing and Bevois Street (Southampton Junction)), flagmen (required where trains crossed public roads) and several clerks, including parcels and station master's clerks, in addition to guards, so when a telephone call came through relating to a member of the staff it was imperative to know who was referred to.

The SM's clerks also dealt with public enquiries and a messenger would stay in that office when awaiting duties. The clerks tried hard to encourage him to answer the telephone but he was always reluctant. On one occasion when he did pick up the telephone, everyone was amazed at how efficient he was. He said 'Yes. Right. I'll pass the message on'. We asked him what the message was and he said that a member of the staff had rung to say that he was unwell and would not be in for work. We congratulated him on his success and asked who it was. 'I didn't ask,' he said; then, with a sudden inspiration, he added 'We will see who doesn't turn up'!

That reminds me of a time, some years later, when I was unwell and, to ensure that a clerk was in the ticket office first thing in the morning, I requested my son to telephone the other clerk at home to ask him to take over my duty. My son started to say 'It's Dad I am ringing up for...', whereupon the other clerk, only half awake on the other end of the telephone, almost passed out on hearing the first two words. Apparently his father had passed away about ten years before and he thought that he was contacting him from the spirit world. Rather odd, he thought, at 5 am and by telephone!

One of our staff came from North Wales and went back periodically for his annual holidays. On one occasion he omitted to contact his relations before setting out. On arrival he found that no one was at home, so turned round and came straight home.

Some parts of the station had suffered bomb damage and few of the upstairs rooms were used; the Old South Western Hotel adjoining was used by the Shipping Department. On the centre of the station concourse was a large pen in which baggage from the Docks was parked. Occasionally

Northam station, just north of Southampton Terminus, looking towards London. The signals on the extreme left relate to the line from Southampton Central to London. The station was served only by trains to and from Terminus. ***Real Photographs***

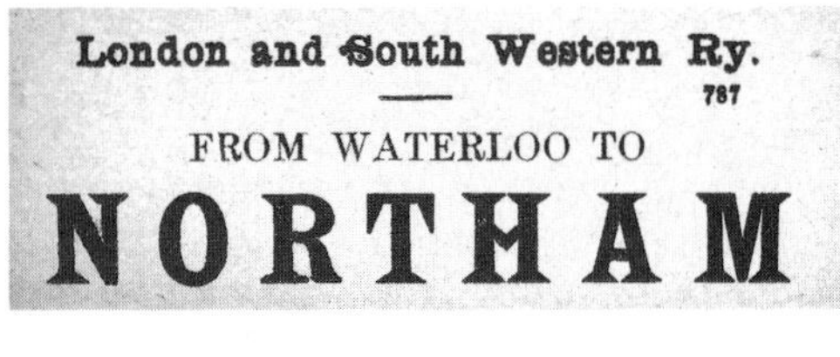

London and South Western Ry.

787

FROM WATERLOO TO

NORTHAM

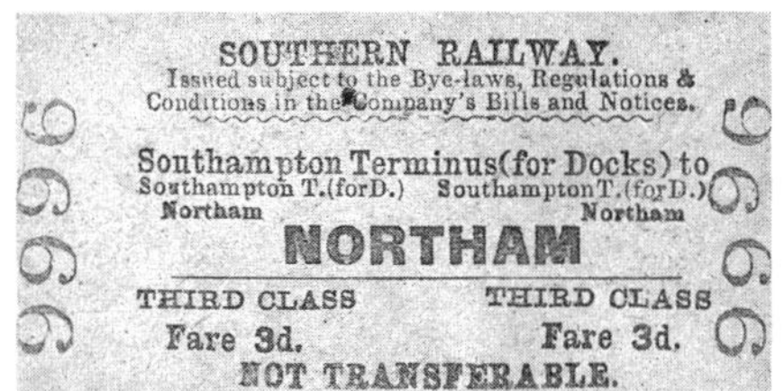

SOUTHERN RAILWAY.

Issued subject to the Bye-laws, Regulations & Conditions in the Company's Bills and Notices.

Southampton Terminus(for Docks) to

Southampton T.(forD.) Northam | SouthamptonT.(forD.) Northam

NORTHAM

THIRD CLASS Fare 3d. | THIRD CLASS Fare 3d.

NOT TRANSFERABLE.

6969

cases and trunks would suddenly disappear and in their place would be rags - apparently 'down and outs' came to the station to restock their wardrobes and changed there and then.

In addition to station work, clerks, ticket collectors and parcels staff would go down to the Docks to meet ocean liners. Some days several boats arrived, while on others perhaps there would be none; in the former instance staff numbers would be stretched to capacity and relief staff would be enlisted to help. I have known boats to offload passengers at any time from 8 am to after midnight. The very largest liners could only arrive when it was high tide, while in some cases passengers would be brought in by tender if only a few were disembarking. Boat trains were timed to run in certain 'pathways' throughout the day; in connection with a particular ship it would be stated that, for example, the 9.35 am and 10.05 am 'pathways' would be used, but should the boat be delayed by fog or gales, trains would then run in later timings. There were a dozen or two of these 'conditional' timings available throughout the day, and on a busy day almost all would be used. I remember more than one instance where so many boat trains were running that some were diverted to Victoria. On occasions we ran direct trains from the Docks to Birmingham or the North of England. If only a handful of

The concourse at Southampton Terminus. ***Lens of Sutton***

passengers disembarked, the docks shunting engine would take a coach of passengers to Southampton Central to be attached to the next up service to Waterloo (sometimes not a very fast train).

Boat train fares were dearer than 'station' fares, so separate ticket stocks were held. In fact, we needed several series of tickets because more than one might be wanted at any one time, the only exception being the 'Mercantile marine on leave' tickets, when fares were always based on station rates as it was not expected that crew members would travel on boat trains. The paying off of crews varied, of course, from ship to ship, and in vessels such as the *Queen Mary* or *Queen Elizabeth* two clerks would be wanted as several hundred men and women might need rail tickets. A tray of tickets would be taken into the docks with rubber stamps, change, fare books, paper ticket books, timetables, etc, remembering that one could not return for reinforcements so all needs had to be taken initially. Sometimes a meal on board was included, after which no one felt like working, least of all returning to the station for a 'late turn'. Generally speaking tickets for crew members were issued by us in the lounge on board. Getting off sometimes proved hazardous as, with such a big vessel, one could easily get lost and, if the tide had turned since you came on, the gangway might be at a different angle to that which it was previously, or perhaps another gangway had been put in from another deck.

Some crew members were entitled to free (full fare) tickets if they were being paid off and sent back to their home port. A member of the Shipping Federation staff would sit beside us and make up a nominal roll to give us, with a warrant or voucher later, to cover

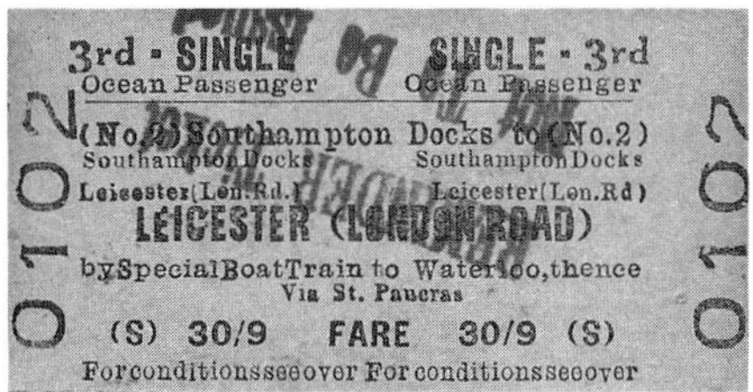

A 'reminder ticket - not to be issued', indicating that new stocks should be ordered. This one is for a boat train journey from Southampton to Leicester (London Rd), via Waterloo and St Pancras.

'Battle of Britain' 'Pacific' No 34071 601 *Squadron* outside the Ocean Terminal building with a boat train. This building had a comparatively short life. *Southern Evening Echo*

Another view of the Terminal building in the 'Old' Docks with an RCTS special hauled by a 'USA' Class 0-6-0T. These strange-looking engines were purchased by the Southern Railway from the US Army Transportation Corps in 1946. *Real Photographs*

the list. At least one relief clerk gave out a dozen or so free tickets to crew before it was realised that these men were not so entitled and should have been sold tickets instead. Our cash balances looked a bit sick that day.

Our tray of tickets would include 'Londons', blank card tickets and a cross section of likely destinations such as Hull, Liverpool, Grimsby, etc. We would bring, maybe, ten or a dozen of each destination, the continuity of numbers being watched, the remainder staying at the station for further use.

Another type of passenger we would get at the docks was troops - troopships were still ferrying servicemen and women in large numbers and these people required free 'forces duty' tickets. These were a print of tickets totally different from anything else and no debit was raised. After a long day's work - all the warrants had to be individually listed - to take no money and to have nothing to show for our hard toil was frustrating.

We could usually enquire which regiment was returning (although many others would be on board) and bring along a preponderance of tickets for that area. I always rued the days when Welsh regiments returned because it was difficult to understand the station names being requested, least of all spell them! When the Hampshire Regiment returned we did, believe it or not, have a warrant offered for a single to Northam (about a mile up the road). By the time he got to the Terminus, waited for a train and walked from the station, he could have been home. Amongst the men from the Scottish regiments were passengers from Auchtermuchty and Pittenweem, and in my ignorance I thought that some of these unlikely names were fictitious, in the same way that some more of the more humorous passengers asked for a ticket to Timbuctoo.

The only shed in the docks with booking offices supplied was the Ocean Terminal. There was a lounge at each end, so a clerk was needed in each, but most passengers had bought tickets through agencies or on board the ship, so those that made their way to us were for the unusual types of tickets, or required a facility not generally available to the public. The ticket racks could be locked up, so when we vacated the lounge after the passengers had gone, cleaners could get in and nothing could be tampered with. A cash balance was made prior to leaving and money, etc, was taken back to the station. The Ocean Terminal had quite a short life, probably no more than 30 years, as boat trains have decreased over the years for various reasons.

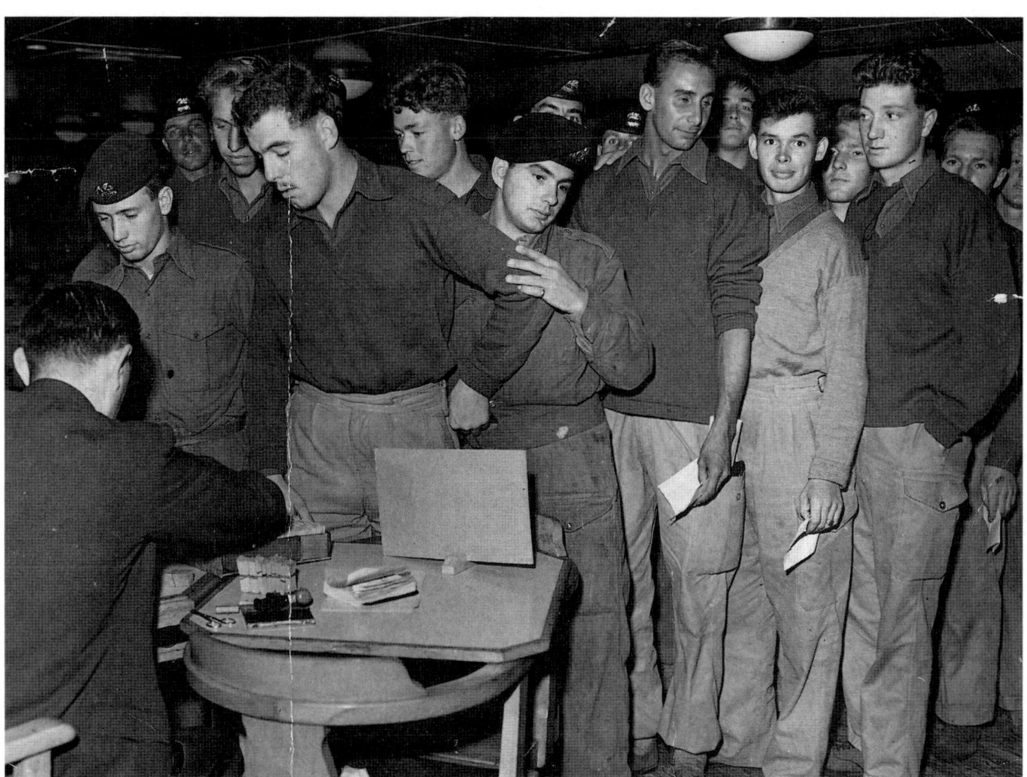

Myself issuing tickets to troops. ***Kentish Express***

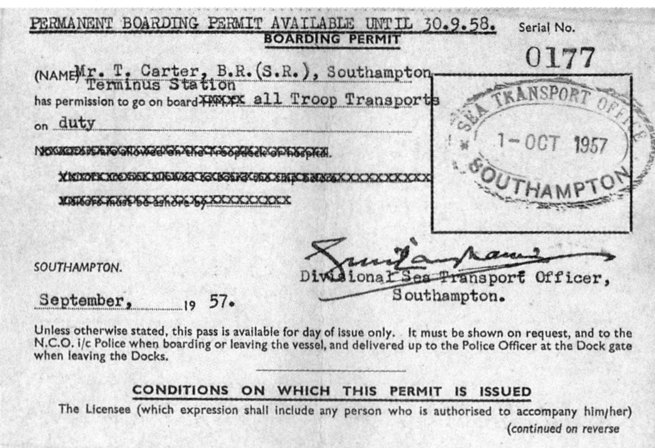

PERMANENT BOARDING PERMIT AVAILABLE UNTIL 30.9.58. Serial No. 0177

BOARDING PERMIT

(NAME) Mr. T. Carter, B.R.(S.R.), Southampton Terminus Station

has permission to go on board all Troop Transports

on duty

SEA TRANSPORT OFFICE 1-OCT 1957 SOUTHAMPTON

SOUTHAMPTON.

September, 19 57.

Divisional Sea Transport Officer, Southampton.

Unless otherwise stated, this pass is available for day of issue only. It must be shown on request, and to the N.C.O. i/c Police when boarding or leaving the vessel, and delivered up to the Police Officer at the Dock gate when leaving the Docks.

CONDITIONS ON WHICH THIS PERMIT IS ISSUED

The Licensee (which expression shall include any person who is authorised to accompany him/her) (continued on reverse

A pass authorising me to board a troopship. Naturally, security had to be enforced.

A 'rebook voucher' was given to passengers who surrendered a voucher but were only booked part of the way, possibly because no through fare was available; it would enable them to buy a reduced-rate ticket for the remainder of their journey.

BRITISH RAILWAYS B.R. 25441/1

REBOOK VOUCHER—FARE PAYABLE AT TIME OF BOOKING

THIS VOUCHER IS NOT TRANSFERABLE AND MUST BE EXCHANGED FOR A TICKET AT THE BOOKING OFFICE, AND IS NOT AVAILABLE FOR TRAVEL BY TRAIN

.... Station .... Region .... 19 ....

The bearer has surrendered .... voucher applying for a ticket at the
(Insert description and number, if any)
.... fare to .... Station
(Insert description of fare chargeable)
but as through fares are not in operation, has been booked to .... Station
only, and on payment of the reduced fare applicable, is entitled to a *FIRST/SECOND Class *SINGLE/RETURN ticket thence to destination

*Delete words not applicable.

Issued by ....
(Signature of Booking Clerk)

IN ALL CASES WHERE RETURN TICKETS ARE ISSUED THE RETURN HALF OF THE TICKET ISSUED AT THE ORIGINAL STARTING POINT MUST BE PRODUCED, ALONG WITH THIS VOUCHER, AT THE REBOOKING STATION.

TO BE FILLED IN AT STATION EXCHANGING VOUCHER.

No. of ticket issued .... Route via ....

Exchange by .... Station
(Signature of Booking Clerk)

NOTES—(a) Rebook vouchers must not be issued for journeys by unauthorised routes.
(b) This voucher must be sent to the Audit Office as authority for the booking.

We had to know what type of passengers would be on each ship and, more important, at which berth it would tie up. We would often play 'Spot the Celebrity', as many well-known faces passed through over the years. For instance, there was no mistaking the very sick Sir Anthony Eden who returned from a cruise hoping to regain his health. Another unmistakable face was that of the irrepressible up-and-coming Tommy Steele. About this time, 'showbiz' personalities often had large fan clubs and on two occasions I saw special trains run from Waterloo full of fans to meet their idol. Such treatment was dealt out to Liberace, the American pianist, and Bill Haley, the 'king of rock 'n' roll', which was then the new craze. The youngsters were excited beyond words; they were kissing the outside of the train and would draw over total strangers to point out their 'hero'. After the trains had left there was an assortment of gloves, shoes, umbrellas, etc, left behind.

The latest time that I ever remember finishing from a ship was 1.30 am. Usually when it was late passengers were given the option of leaving straight away or staying on board another night; thus perhaps one train would run late at night and the other the next morning. I found this job to be one of experience. At first I was completely baffled but, after a while, one could remember by previous arrivals what to expect from a given ship, how many clerks would be needed, what type of foreign currency would be acceptable, etc.

The ships were all different. If they were not berthing at the Ocean Terminal, we would take the boat train fare tickets to the ship with us; we had five sets of these. In the unlikely event of more than five clerks working, or more than five ships arriving at once, a bundle of tickets would have to be split up and possibly some tickets unavoidably issued out of sequence. It was not unusual to have money owing by the shipping agents, as their representative would suddenly ask for a ticket for a special passenger and give you a letterhead or label bearing their name, to whom the account had to be rendered. It was quite commonplace to accept Canadian and US dollars and travellers cheques and Australian and New Zealand banknotes, amongst other things.

Away from the Terminal, a sentry-box-type structure would be provided in the customs' shed (provided, if you were lucky, with a light and heater). Tickets would be issued through a small grill with a very dirty ledge, a far cry from the carpeted Terminal. About this time a facility existed whereby passengers could buy coupons in the States and exchange them for tickets in this country. When booking some ships, there were more coupons taken than money. On returning to the station, the clerk had to account for these by counting them. As far as I can recall they were of two values - 6d (2½p) and 2s 6d (12½p) - so, as they were only about 1 inch square, they were easily lost, and several pages had to be extracted at a time for high-price tickets.

Another shipping line had the arrangement that we accepted the passengers' shipping tickets (instead of cash) for a rail ticket, and the shipping agent would pay the account. These passage tickets were almost foolscap size, so we returned to the station with as much paper as we could carry, and then came the fun of making a cash balance. There was, for example, no reason to suppose that the shipping line made the same age limit for children's fares as we did, so a passenger's ship ticket might be for one adult passenger and one child whereas, in fact, we had to issue two adult fares. Again, a passage ticket might be for three passengers but one of them might not travel by train, so the counting of passengers for accountancy purposes was not easy.

During my period at Southampton, West Indian immigrants were arriving in large numbers and this was one of the few occasions when boat trains ran to destinations other than London. I felt very sorry for the passengers, as many had no warm clothes and were not really sure where they were going as they had never realised the size of our cities and how difficult it would be to find their relatives when they arrived, possibly not knowing the full address.

Naturally they were very cautious and counted out their money very slowly for fear of being swindled. A large number of transactions were paid for in silver, in fact very old coins, and how I now wish I had bought out more of the very old Victorian coins, as I did not appreciate then how much their value would increase. I still have the oldest coin which I took - a William IV shilling! As you can imagine, booking these ships was a very slow process and making a cash balance took equally as long as there was so much change to count.

Although working at the Terminus was very different, time became long as the station itself was not busy, and on overtime one had to go to the Docks where long periods of waiting were often necessary. Already there were signs that the station would not last much longer and much of our time was spent in writing out fare books for the docks and other routine tasks. When attending ships there were considerable periods when they were delayed by fog or gales, and I never knew really when I would be off duty. So change was in the air again.

8.
STEYNING 1959-64
I The line and its traffic

My colleague in the ticket office was thinking of applying for his station master's rules examination which would enable him to apply for SM posts. I decided to follow suit and we had a stiff verbal test of the Rule Book, Signalling Regulations, and items from the General Appendix. Signalling and rules classes are held at various centres in the winter evenings or by correspondence, and I had taken these from time to time. It was then a matter of patience in applying for station master positions as they became vacant. I knew only too well that it meant moving house yet again and going back to a house above a station.

After an interview at Redhill Divisional Office in 1959 I was appointed as Station Master at Steyning in Sussex. I was also in charge of Bramber and Henfield, and when 'on call' was responsible for the whole branch line.

My introduction to the town was not a pleasant one, though the circumstances were entirely of my own making. On our first investigation of Steyning station I parked my car in the High Street and asked someone the way to the station. They pointed along Church Street and we found it to be a lengthy walk. By the time we had talked to a member of the staff and looked at the house, a considerable period of time had elapsed, and, on returning to our car, found that someone had parked opposite it, the traffic was snarled up and a policeman had been called to control the congestion. I received a summons but, after a written apology from me, I was let off with a small fine.

Soon after being appointed I was selected to attend a residential course at Derby. There were lectures on commercial and operating subjects and visits to depots but the climax of the course was operating the model railway which ran round the perimeter of the hall. The only disadvantage was that the layout was complicated and by the time one had accustomed oneself to the timetable and stock working one's turn was over. To make it more realistic, the clock went at double the normal speed and the models travelled from one station to another at greatly reduced speed; thus a more realistic timetable was operated. If a vehicle became derailed, the tool van and crane had to be called up and emergency measures put in, and only then was normal service resumed with the obvious time lag.

Back at Steyning I was anxious to put my knowledge into use but was still petrified that, should some major incident occur, I would not be able to cope. I felt that those whose first station was in the suburban area had an enormous disadvantage as they were certainly 'in at the deep end'. After a while, however, I began to feel more confident and knew that whatever emergency came along, I would find a way out.

The station house was not very convenient. Downstairs was a kitchen, dining room and bathroom (very much in need of decoration), with three bedrooms and a sitting room upstairs, all leading off a long passage. This proved difficult when moving our furniture in, as with a winding staircase and low ceilings, most of the furniture had to be brought in through a bedroom window.

This meant that unloading our things ran

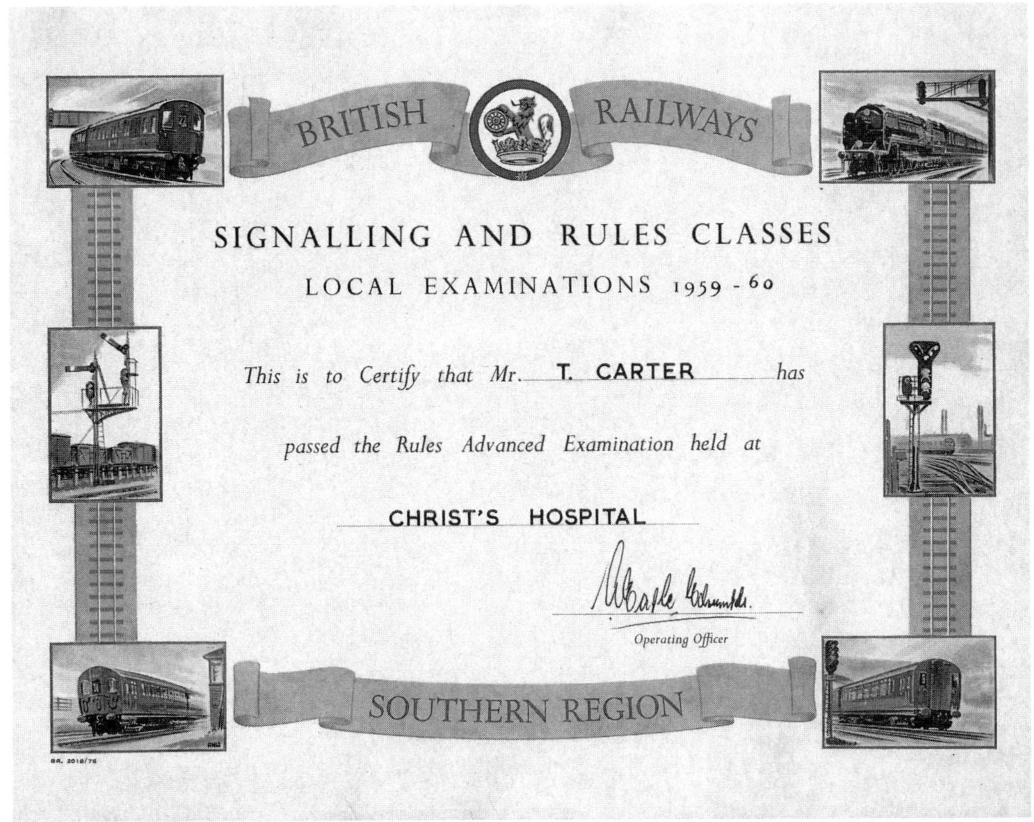

BRITISH RAILWAYS

SIGNALLING AND RULES CLASSES

LOCAL EXAMINATIONS 1959 - 60

This is to Certify that Mr. T. CARTER *has*

passed the Rules Advanced Examination held at

CHRIST'S HOSPITAL

Operating Officer

SOUTHERN REGION

BR. 2018/76

Evening classes were held at various centres throughout the Region, but Christ's Hospital seems an unlikely venue!

over into a second day; luckily we had made arrangements to stay the night elsewhere, or it might have been difficult! We had a front door opening on to the road and a back door opening on to the platform, which was convenient, but callers invariably came to both doors thinking that it was two houses.

Steyning is a charming market town and we enjoyed living there and felt that we 'belonged'. I got involved with life in the town helping with youth work, etc. My parents still lived in Worthing, although my father was now retired, so we were not totally strange to the neighbourhood.

We acquired a poodle shortly after our arrival and my cousin brought her by car from Hampshire one Sunday. His young son threw open the car door upon arrival and the dog was gone. As I was not yet very conversant with the area and my cousin and the dog knew it even less, we thought we had a problem. However, after 20 or 30 minutes of searching people's farms, barns and gardens, we eventually located and brought her home. This was the first of several wanderings for her as my children, still small, could never remember to close the door behind them, so she would wander off, ignoring all calls. Fortunately she never caused an accident or was never involved in one, but she would bathe in the slime at the side of the track and be brought in smelling rather unpleasant and in need of a bath. She had to make regular visits to a poodle parlour at Brighton, but I made certain that my first visit was also my last. Upon collecting her on the first occasion I vowed that this duty would never be mine again as the appearance and perfume of the dog was beyond belief. I think I preferred the muddy slime smell!

Steyning in the snow, January 1960. It is difficult to trace the station today - the back of the Brighton-bound (down) platform remains, but on what is now a bypass road. *D. V. Morgan*

A market was held outside the station once a week and we did quite big business with car parking for the customers. Furniture sales were also held periodically and the trains virtually emptied out on those days. When the passengers returned in the afternoons carrying their wares, including live and dead poultry, the station did not look quite as clean as it did before they arrived.

We undertook parcel deliveries to the local area each morning and in the country districts in the afternoons. One day a tin of fisherman's maggots booked as 'parcels' traffic was received by train. The leading porter concerned left it in the warm office overnight and the following day there was a carpet of them on the office floor; in fact, we were plagued by flies for some time to come. The freight yard was open when I first went there and we would receive trucks of coal, fertiliser, livestock, bricks, etc; we always received more loaded wagons than we sent away, but there was a period when we were sending agricultural implements to Ireland.

I found some of the other practices strange. Stations do tend to get involved in businesses disassociated with railways and Steyning was no exception. Most stations would be agencies for insurance whereby passengers could insure their baggage or themselves for a journey, and also motor car and house insurance was undertaken with the same firm at favourable rates. As there was a considerable amount of farmland nearby, farmers came to us to borrow sacks for harvesting, as we were also agents for the West of England Sack Co. It was inevitable that this attracted vermin as often grains of corn were left in the used sacks which would remain on the platform, or 'stage', in the goods shed until there was enough to make up a wagonload.

A most unusual derailment occurred in the goods shed one day. The wagons were running under their own power into the shed at walking pace and one touched a bundle of sacks protruding from the stage. The leading bogie immediately became derailed, I imagine due to the very low speed, but the permanent way staff rerailed it by means of jacks.

Private sidings were provided at Beeding for the local cement works and the signal box there was switched in about four times a day for coal and cement trains; for supervision purposes, the sidings came under the station master at Shoreham-by-Sea. This siding continued in use well after the branch closed.

The first station up the line from Shoreham was Bramber; this was the only station lit by electricity and the buildings were almost identical to those at Southwater and Partridge Green. Bramber had no sidings and had possessed no signal box for many years. Any rainfall seemed immediately to bring the station toilets into a state of flood, and although men came on several occasions to remedy the matter, no permanent solution was found until one day a worker who was determined not to be beaten brought a pneumatic drill and began to probe deeper. He dug up the floor of the lavatory, followed the pipes under the wall, dug up the approach road, following the pipes into the garden of the station house where an employee lived, dug up his garden and finished up under his chicken house, where he found a cess pit which was full and had been for years. The cess pit was emptied. End of problem.

Next came Steyning, only half a mile away and lit by gas. When all the lamps were alight the sound resembled an orchestra tuning up. There had been a clerk at Steyning when I first went there, as there was at Henfield, the next station, which was also gas-lit, but in later years the platform staff performed the office work and also signalling and shunting. All the other stations were lit by Tilley lamps.

Partridge Green followed Henfield and here the sidings remained well after the others had been taken up. West Grinstead came next. Passengers were always few and far between there, but the National Stud provided us with a regular supply of horses for despatch. Southwater was the sixth station, and was the only one to have no footbridge or subway; at the 'country' end of the station on the up side were situated private sidings belonged to the local brick company. An extra member of staff was provided at these last three stations for shunting, number-taking and cleaning lamps.

Bramber looking south in April 1961. Note the long platform and canopy on the down side, dating back to the days when special trains ran to the castle (or what was left of it!). The numerous luggage barrows were used daily for market-garden produce to London markets. The signal in view is the Steyning up distant, the stations being only about half a mile apart. *Shoreham Herald*

Bramber, looking towards Steyning, before electric light was installed. The gas lamps had to be removed because the pipes ran between the two parts of the double road bridge and were inaccessible. *Real Photographs*

An up (northbound) RCTS special at Henfield, possibly returning to Reading, behind ex-LB&SCR 'K' Class 'Mogul' No 32353. In some respects Henfield station was of a similar design to Steyning. *Lens of Sutton*

Partridge Green. The loco is propelling a Horsham-Brighton train. *Real Photographs*

London Brighton and South Coast Railway.

Partridge Green to

St. Leonard's

An up van train approaching Partridge Green from the south. Note the signal on the 'wrong' side of the line, to aid sighting. *Collector Cards*

West Grinstead. Situated on the A272 but never attracting much passenger traffic, it was nonetheless often the winner of the 'Best Kept Station' competition. It is difficult to know when this photograph was taken as the station did not alter for years, except that upper quadrant signals were used latterly. When a television film set during the First World War was made there, the signal arms were replaced with lower quadrants for the purpose. *Real Photographs*

West Grinstead and Steyning both won awards in the 1962 'Best Kept Station' competition. Bramber appears to have missed out that year, but it was often a winner with its rose trees round the entrance; standard of book-keeping was also taken into consideration.

BRITISH RAILWAYS : SOUTHERN REGION,
LINE MANAGER (Central Division)
ESSEX HOUSE, CROYDON.

Ref: R.12/P.430 26th February, 1963.

AWARDS FOR BEST KEPT STATIONS, 1962.

I have pleasure in announcing the results of the above competition for the year ended September 1962. Date, time and place of presentations will be advised to prize-winners as soon as Certificates and posters are received.

Particulars of the prize winning Stations and Depots and the awards which will be made are given hereunder and I should like to take this opportunity of expressing my appreciation of the interest in this competition displayed by all members of the staff.

STATIONS.

CLASS "A"			
	First Prize	£18.	LEWES
	Second Prize	£12.	HORSHAM.
CLASS "B"			
	First Prize	£14	POLEGATE
	Second Prize	£10.	HURST GREEN
	Third Prize	£7.	GATWICK AIRPORT.
CLASS "C"			
	First Prize	£10	GROOMBRIDGE
	Second Prize	£8.	LINGFIELD
	Third Prize	£5.	BRIDGE
	Two additonal Third Prizes	£5.	OXTED
		£5.	GIPSY HILL.
CLASS "D"			
	First Prize	£8.	FALMER
	Second Prize	£6.	STEYNING
	Third Prize	£4.	CRANLEIGH
	Two additional Third Prizes	£4.	CHIPSTEAD
		£4.	GORING-BY-SEA
CLASS "E"			
	First Prize	£6.	BAYNARDS
	Second Prize	£4.	BALCOMBE
	Third Prize	£3.	BRAMLEY
	Four additional Third Prizes	£3.	ASHURST
		£3.	WEST GRINSTEAD
		£3.	ISFIELD
		£3.	GODSTONE

Southwater. This was the only station on the line with no footbridge. In the background the main road crosses the railway, while the entrance to the sidings can be seen in the foreground by the foot crossing. *Collector Cards*

'C2X' Class 0-6-0 No 32527 with an up Hove-Three Bridges freight near Southwater in March 1959. *John Scrace*

No 31276, one of the popular 'H' Class Wainwright SE&CR 0-4-4 tanks, at Itchingfield Junction between Southwater and Christ's Hospital with the 16.30 Brighton-Horsham in April 1960. *John Scrace*

The front of Christ's Hospital station in Southern days. *Real Photographs*

'Hampshire' DEMU unit No 1113 forms the 15.30 Horsham-Brighton train at Itchingfield Junction in March 1965. *John Scrace*

The only other station before Horsham was Christ's Hospital which was interesting in that this enormous place had its own station master and was lit entirely by Tilley lamps; one man on each turn had to attend to seven platforms, clean and trim the lamps, collect tickets, see passengers across the line to and from the Guildford trains, give to and collect from the driver of that train the 'staff and ticket' (as the single line was worked under that arrangement), operate the ground frame as required, in addition to dealing with two trains per hour each way on the Mid Sussex line and one train each way hourly via Steyning. Christ's Hospital is still open today, being served by electric services via Arundel.

The signalling at Steyning was Harper's block; it was the requirement that the station master held 'a working knowledge of the box' and I had to switch the box into circuit on several occasions. The section from Old Shoreham bridge to Itchingfield Junction, just south of Christ's Hospital, was just adequate for an hourly service, but if, for instance, a light engine was put through it was necessary to break up the section to prevent delay to the following train, as only one train must be in a section in one direction at any one time. The problem then arose of being able to switch out again after the passage of the engine. This could only be done when there was no train in the section. Steyning box was switched in for most of the day on weekdays, while the others came in and out from time to time as I will explain later. More than once passengers were heard to say 'It is chaps like you who cause accidents by not operating the signals', but of course the principle of one train in a section stands however long or short the section, and the signals of a 'closed' box must be left in the clear position, although, on a single line (which this was not), signals in both directions showing 'proceed' do look odd!

The staff at the stations were good. In addition to knowing office work they had to know shunting and signalling at all except Bramber, clean signal lamps and do general parcels and goods work, including folding and returning wagon sheets, cleaning out used wagons and doing station cleaning. The daily wagon return was a bit of a puzzler. The compiler had to try and estimate how many wagons would be emptied within the next 24 hours, in addition to listing the station's requirements. Each type of wagon had a title and a different code letter was used for those expected to be empty, definitely empty, required, etc. When reading this over the telephone to the wagon control, it sounded like a foreign language.

We had one of the coldest winters as well as one of the hottest summers for many years while I was there. The cold brought its problems; although the steam service continued to run fairly well, the electric coastal service was badly affected. One day when the snow was very deep a train was stuck and the guard walked along the track to get assistance. Where our line joined the coast line his footprints suddenly stopped and we feared that he had had an accident and had slipped down the bank. We searched all around, but it transpired that the reason why his steps could no longer be found was that a light engine had picked him up!

It was my first summer at Steyning when the sun shone day after day and we had no rain for weeks; everything was very dry and engines were constantly setting the banks alight with sparks. Sometimes a corn field would go up in smoke, to the annoyance of the local farmer. I soon made his acquaintance! If the staff could not cope with the outbreak we would summon the brigade, but these men were only part time and first had to get to the fire station; sometimes they would be busy elsewhere, and bearing in mind that some of these places were very inaccessible by road, often much damage was done.

The train service was hourly on weekdays with slight variations in the morning and evening peak. They were push-and-pull and the usual motive power was a Drummond 'M7' or Wainwright 'H' Class 0-4-4 tank, the latter being very popular with the drivers. The coaches were old LB&SCR or LSWR stock but were later replaced by Maunsell sets numbered in the 600 series; these were two Maunsell coaches - an Open Second and a Corridor Composite with toilets removed - and a third non-corridor coach, adapted for push-pull working.

This necessitated staff becoming familiar with 'buck-eye' couplings for the first time. As loco-hauled trains travelled with the 'buck-eye' down (unlike multiple unit stock) a piece of bent gas pipe was always kept handy to lift the coupling, as its weight could easily do anyone an injury if lifted wrongly. The piece of piping could be used to enable a swinging movement to be made.

There were well over a hundred school children arriving at Steyning each morning and returning at night, and quite a few commuters used the station; they could change at Horsham or Hove or Brighton for London, although the cheapest fare was via Horsham. On Saturdays football fans went to Hove and shoppers to Brighton; the trains were often full and the brake van would be packed to capacity with prams. We had one through train from London Bridge to Brighton via Horsham each weekday, usually hauled by a

Table 30 — HORSHAM, SHOREHAM-BY-SEA AND BRIGHTON

Miles	Down — Week Days	am	am	am	am	am	am	am	am	pm	pm SX	pm SO	pm SX	pm SO	pm	pm SX	pm SO	pm SO
	LONDON																	
	78 Victoria dep			5*20	7 1	8 0	9 18	10 18	11 18	12 18	1 2	1 18	2 2	2 18	3 18	4 18	4 18	5 18
	78 London Bridge "			5‡ 8	6*59		9†K12	10†SX8	11 0	12T 0	12C53	12T55	1C53	2 0	3T 0	4† 6	3†53	4†53
	78 Waterloo "			5C16	6B46	8②16	9②36	10D 5	11D 5	12G 5	1②35	1H 6	2②35	2H 5	3②35	4H 6	4H 5	5H 5
—	Horsham dep	6 19		7 19	8 15	9 19	10 19	11 19	12 19	1 19	2 19	2 19	3 19	3 19	4 19	5 19	5 19	6 19
2	Christ's Hospital W	6 23		7 23	8 19	9 23	10 23	11 23	12 23	1 23	2 23	2 23	3 23	3 23	4 23	5 23	5 23	6 23
4	Southwater	6 29		7 29	8 25	9 29	10 29	11 29	12 29	1 29	2 29	2 29	3 29	3 29	4 29	5 29	5 29	6 29
7	West Grinstead	6 36		7 36	8 32	9 36	10 36	11 36	12 36	1 36	2 36	2 36	3 36	3 36	4 36	5 36	5 36	6 36
9	Partridge Green	6 42		7 43	8 38	9 42	10 42	11 42	12 42	1 42	2 42	2 42	3 42	3 42	4 42	5 42	5 42	6 42
11	Henfield	6 47		7 48	8 43	9 47	10 47	11 47	12 47	1 47	2 47	2 47	3 47	3 47	4 47	5 47	5 47	6 47
15	Steyning	6 56	7 36	7 58	8 52	9 56	10 56	11 56	12 56	1 56	2 56	2 56	3 56	3 56	4 56	5 56	5 56	6 56
16	Bramber	6 59	7 38	8 1	8 55	9 59	10 59	11 59	12 59	1 59	2 59	2 59	3 59	3 59	4 59	5 59	5 59	6 59
20	Shoreham-by-Sea	7 8	7 47	8 10	9 5	10 8	11 8	12 8	1 8	2 8	3 8	3 8	4 8	4 8	5 8	6 8	6 8	7 8
21½	Southwick	[illegible]	7 51		9 9													
22½	Fishersgate Halt																	
23	Portslade & West Hove	[illegible]	7 54	8 16	9 13													
24	Aldrington Halt																	
24½	Hove	7 16	7 58	8 20	9 17	10 17	11 17	12 17	1 17	2 17	3 17	3 17	4 17	4 17	5 17	6 17	6 17	7 17
26	Brighton arr	7 23	8 2	8 24	9 22	10 22	11 21	12 22	1 22	2 21	3 21	3 21	4 21	4 21	5 22	6 21	6 21	7 21

Down	Week Days—continued pm SX	pm SX	pm SO	pm SX	pm SO	pm	pm SO	Sundays am	am	am	am	pm	pm	pm	pm	pm	pm
LONDON																	
78 Victoria dep	5 29	6 10	6 2	7 10	7 18	8 2	9 10	7 2	8 2	9 10	11 10	1 2	3 10	4 2	5 2	7 10	8 2
78 London Bridge "	5 14	5 47	5C53	7 0	6†53	7†53	8†53		7②55	8†55	10†54	12T30	2†55	3T30	4T30	6†55	7T30
78 Waterloo "	5H 6	6②36	6②35	7H 5	7H 5	8②35	9H 5		8C 2	9F 2	11F 2	12②42	3F 2	3②42	4②42	7F 2	7②42
Horsham dep	6 26	7 19	7 19	8 19	8 19	9 19	10 19	8 19	9 19	10 19	12 19	2 19	4 19	5 19	6 19	8 19	9 19
Christ's Hospital W		7 23	7 23	8 23	8 23	9 23	10 23	8 23	9 23	10 23	12 23	2 23	4 23	5 23	6 23	8 23	9 23
Southwater	6 33	7 29	7 29	8 29	8 29	9 29	10 29	8 29	9 29	10 29	12 29	2 29	4 29	5 29	6 29	8 29	9 29
West Grinstead	6 40	7 36	7 36	8 36	8 36	9 36	10 36	8 36	9 36	10 36	12 36	2 36	4 36	5 36	6 36	8 36	9 36
Partridge Green	6 46	7 42	7 42	8 42	8 42	9 42	10 42	8 42	9 42	10 42	12 42	2 42	4 42	5 42	6 42	8 42	9 42
Henfield	6 51	7 47	7 47	8 47	8 47	9 47	10 47	8 47	9 47	10 47	12 47	2 47	4 47	5 47	6 47	8 47	9 47
Steyning	7 1	7 56	7 56	8 56	8 56	9 56	10 56	8 57	9 57	10 57	12 57	2 57	4 57	5 57	6 57	8 57	9 57
Bramber	7 4	7 59	7 59	8 59	8 59	9 59		8 59	9 59	10 59	12 59	2 59	4 59	5 59	6 59	8 59	9 59
Shoreham-by-Sea	7 14	8 8	8 8	9 8	9 0	10 8	11 7	9 9	10 9	11 9	1 9	3 9	5 9	6 9	7 9	9 9	10 9
Southwick																	
Fishersgate Halt																	
Portslade & West Hove																	
Aldrington Halt																	
Hove	7 23	8 17	8 17	9 17	9 17	10 17	11 16	9 17	10 17	11 17	1 17	3 17	5 17	6 17	7 17	9 17	10 17
Brighton arr	7 27	8 21	8 21	9 21	9 21	10 21	11 20	9 21	10 21	11 21	1 21	3 21	5 21	6 21	7 21	9 21	10 21

② Second class only
* Change at East Croydon
† Second class only. Change at Sutton
B Mondays to Fridays. Dep 6 30 am on Saturdays only. Change at Epsom. Second class only
C Second class only. Change at Epsom
D Second class only. Change at Dorking North. Dep 1 minute later on Saturdays
F Second class only. Change at Epsom and Dorking North
‡ 14 minutes later on Saturdays
G Second class only. Dep 12 6 pm on Saturdays
H Second class only. Change at Dorking North
K 3 minutes later on Mondays to Fridays
SO or S0 Saturdays only
SX or SX Mondays to Fridays
T Second class only. Change at East Croydon
W Christ's Hospital, West Horsham
x Also dep 5 25 am; change at Three Bridges

For COMPLETE SERVICE between Shoreham-by-Sea and Brighton, see Table 28

For OTHER TRAINS between Horsham and Christ's Hospital, see Tables 20 and 31

Table 30—continued — BRIGHTON, SHOREHAM-BY-SEA AND HORSHAM

Miles	Up — Week Days	am	am	am	am	am	am	pm SX	pm SO	pm SO	pm SX	pm SX	pm SO	pm	pm SX	pm	pm	pm SX	pm SO	pm SX	pm SO
—	Brighton dep	6 30	7 30	8 0	9 30	10 30	11 37	12 30	12 30	1 27	1 30	2 30	2 30	3 30	3 59	4 30	5 30	6 13	6 30	7 14	7 30
1½	Hove	6 34	7 35	8 4	9 35	10 35	11 41	12 35	12 35	1 31	1 35	2 35	2 35	3 35	4 3	4 35	5 35	6 17	6 35	7 18	7 35
2	Aldrington Halt																				
3	Portslade & West Hove	6 38	7 39	8 8						1 35							5SX39	6 21		7 22	
3½	Fishersgate Halt																				
4½	Southwick	6 41		8 12						1 39								6 25			
6	Shoreham-by-Sea	6 44	7 44	8 16	9 44	10 44	11 54	12 44	12 44	1 44	1 44	2 44	2 44	3 44	4 12	4 44	5 44	6 29	6 44	7 28	7 44
10	Bramber	6 53	7 53	8 25	9 53	10 53	12 3	12 53	12 53	1 53	1 53	2 53	2 53	3 53	4 21	4 53	5 53	6 38	6 53	7 37	7 53
10½	Steyning	6 58	7A58	8 28	9A58	10A58	12 8	12A58	12A58	1A58	1A58	2A58	2A58	3A58	4 24	4A58	5A58	6 41	6A58	7G48	7A58
14½	Henfield	7 6	8 6	8 37	10 6	11 6	12 16	1 6	1 6	2 6	2 6	3 6	3 6	4 6	4 32	5 6	6 6	6 50	7 6	7 55	8 6
16½	Partridge Green	7 11	8 11	8 42	10 11	11 11	12 22	1 11	1 11	2 11	2 11	3 11	3 11	4 11	4 37	5 11	6 11	6 55	7 11	8 1	8 11
18½	West Grinstead	7 16	8 16	8 47	10 16	11 16	12 28	1 16	1 16	2 16	2 16	3 16	3 16	4 16	4 43	5 16	6 16	7 1	7 16	8 8	8 16
21½	Southwater	7 23	8 23	8 54	10 23	11 23	12 35	1 23	1 23	2 23	2 23	3 23	3 23	4 23	4 49	5 23	6 23	7 8	7 23	8 16	8 23
23½	Christ's Hospital W	7 28	8 28	8 59	10 28	11 28	12 40	1 28	1 28	2 28	2 28	3 28	3 28	4 28	4 54	5 28	6SO28	7 13	7 28	8 22	8 28
26	Horsham arr	7 32	8 32	9 3	10 32	11 32	12 45	1 32	1 32	2 32	2 32	3 32	3 32	4 32	5 0	5 32	6 33	7 18	7 32	8 28	8 32
	LONDON																				
61½	78 Waterloo arr	9②4	10H 3	10J44	12D 6	10 6	2②36	3②36	3②36	4②6	4②6	5②3	5②6	6B 3	6H23	7F 4	8②6	8C44	9②6	10②6	10②6
63½	78 London Bridge "	8*43	9*32	9E57	11T51	1†13	2*36	3†11	3†13	4†13	4† 3	5† 2			6②22		8*36	8②44	9†13	10†13	10†13
63½	78 Victoria "	8 37	9 31	10 18	11‡40	12‡40	2 15	2 46	2 40	3 40	3 40	4 40	4 46	5‡40	6 15	6 40	7 46	8 40	8 40	9 40	9 40

Up	Week Days—continued pm	pm	pm SX	pm SO	Sundays am	am	am	am	pm	pm	pm	pm	pm	pm
Brighton dep	8 30	9 30	10 30	10 30	7 30	9 30	10 30	11 30	1 30	3 30	5 30	6 30	7 30	9 30
Hove	8 35	9 35	10 35	10 35	7 35	9 35	10 35	11 35	1 35	3 35	5 35	6 35	7 35	9 35
Aldrington Halt														
Portslade & West Hove			10 38	10 38										
Fishersgate Halt														
Southwick			10 42	10 42										
Shoreham-by-Sea	8 44	9 44	10 45	10 45	7 44	9 44	10 44	11 44	1 44	3 44	5 44	6 44	7 44	9 44
Bramber	8 53	9 53	10 55	10 55	7 53	9 53	10 53	11 53	1 53	3 53	5 53	6 53	7 53	9 53
Steyning	8A58	9A58	10 58	10 59	7A58	9A58	10A58	11A58	1A58	3A58	5A58	6A58	7A58	9A58
Henfield	9 6	10 6		11 8	8 6	10 6	11 6	12 6	2 6	4 6	6 6	7 6	8 6	10 6
Partridge Green	9 11	10 11		11 13	8 11	10 11	11 11	12 11	2 11	4 11	6 11	7 11	8 11	10 11
West Grinstead	9 16	10 15		11 18	8 16	10 16	11 16	12 16	2 16	4 16	6 16	7 16	8 16	10 16
Southwater	9 23	10 23		11 25	8 23	10 23	11 23	12 23	2 23	4 23	6 23	7 23	8 23	10 23
Christ's Hospital W	9 28	10 28		11 30	8 28	10 28	11 28	12 28	2 28	4 28	6 28	7 28	8 28	10 28
Horsham arr	9 32	10 32		11 34	8 32	10 32	11 32	12 32	2 32	4 32	6 32	7 32	8 32	10 32
LONDON														
78 Waterloo arr	11②6	12K11			9C54	12②3	1②3	2②3	4②3	6②3	8②3	9②3	10②3	12②6
78 London Bridge "	10T51				9②50	12† 3	1T10	2T10	4T10	6† 3	8† 3	9† 3	10† 3	
78 Victoria "	10‡46	11 52			9 47	11 43	12 47	1 46	3 46	5 43	7 43	8 43	9 43	11 51

② Second class only
* Change at East Croydon
† Second class only. Change at Sutton
‡ Arr 3 minutes earlier
B Second class only. Change at Dorking North on Mondays to Fridays. Arr 6②6 pm on Saturdays
C Second class only. Change at Epsom
D Second class only. Arr 3 minutes earlier on Saturdays
E Arr 10T31 am on Saturdays
F Second class only. Arr 7 6 pm on Saturdays
G Arr 7 minutes earlier
H Second class only. Change at Dorking North
J Second class only. Change at Epsom. Arr 10②42 am on Saturdays
J 2 minutes later on Mondays to Fridays
K Second class only. Change at Wimbledon
N Second class only. On Saturdays arr 9②43 am
SO or S0 Saturdays only
SX or SX Mondays to Fridays
T Second class only. Change at East Croydon
W Christ's Hospital, West Horsham

For COMPLETE SERVICE between Brighton and Shoreham-by-Sea, see Table 28

For OTHER TRAINS between Christ's Hospital and Horsham, see Tables 28 and 31

The steam service on the Steyning line, probably *circa* 1960. The only through train was the 05.08 London Bridge-Brighton (weekdays), although this is not made clear. The type was set up including all the Halts, but they need not have bothered!

Maunsell push-and-pull set No 601 approaching Steyning, the propelling loco at the rear. ***D. V. Morgan***

'West Country' 'Pacific'. This service had several vans on the rear and brought our parcels down from London for delivery. I well recall one day when the loco was gaining time all the way down and was early by the time it reached our station; as the guard was unaware of the situation, the train left each station before the staff could get out on to the platform, and it got as far as Bramber before the staff were able to speak to the guard. There it had a long wait for 'time' and there were many disgruntled passengers that day. This service ceased to operate when dieselisation came.

We had our batch of humorists amongst the passengers, as every station has, and one elderly man would always say 'Where is the buffet car today?' or 'Is there a Pullman?' From time to time I was able to point out that there was one as sometimes empty stock *en route* for Lancing Works would come down on the rear of our trains to be 'specialed' from Brighton to Lancing.

I never ceased to be amazed at how often passengers got on the wrong train. As ours was the only steam service at Shoreham-by-Sea, how could anyone go wrong? But time and time again I saw passengers alight at Bramber who had gone from Steyning to Shoreham to change for Worthing, and had got on the next train only to arrive back up on the branch again.

As the service deteriorated and became less reliable, we persuaded the Divisional Manager that something better must be tried, so the 'P&P' working was abolished. This now meant that any rolling-stock could be used, and any loco which was permitted to run on that line could, in theory, be used. Gradually the 'M7s' and 'Hs' were replaced by Midland 'Teddy Bear' Class 2 or BR Class 4 tanks. Some branch lines had run without guards, but ours was not one, probably due to the fact that it ran over stretches of main line at each end, unlike some rural branches. The experiment was tried between Three Bridges and East Grinstead, but there were problems, one of which was the remitting of traffic cash for banking as there was no guard to sign for it. At least one of these cash bags disappeared without trace - they were thrown into a locked brake van and at the other end were either forgotten or probably finished up inside an open-ended package such as a box of plants and the recipient was the richer. (Takings were probably small anyway, but the necessary reporting caused a lot of work and trouble.)

II Scenes from station life - and a centenary

Let me return to the position as it was when I went to Steyning. A water column was provided at the departure end of each platform and engines would invariably draw water on every trip. When proceeding to Brighton the engine would be propelling, so it could only take water by pushing the train set beyond the platform so that the engine was beside the water column. Passengers would arrive late whilst it was filling up and would expect to be allowed to join the train. The more athletic passengers could just manage to join it by climbing into the rearmost compartment from the platform slope. Some drivers would actually set back again for them to get in. Passengers were caught out from time to time when they relied on the train stopping for water, and were indignant when water was not required and they missed the train when it did not halt beyond the platform. Schoolchildren were often the worst offenders as they finished school only a few minutes before the train time and had to run all the way to the station - it was not unusual for perhaps 20 or 25 boys to travel in the last compartment from Steyning to Bramber and move up the train there. On more than one occasion some boys were left behind at Bramber because they took too long to find another compartment and the train left without them.

In later years the 10.19 pm Horsham-Brighton and 10.30 pm Brighton-Horsham (booked to run on Saturdays only) were discontinued for economy reasons. These were non-standard in that they were not booked to stop at Bramber and Southwater respectively. Christ's Hospital was served by all trains except the 6.26 pm (SX) Horsham-Brighton. West Grinstead was closed on Sundays in later years. There was a service starting at Steyning at 7.35 am (weekdays) for Brighton and a 10.34 pm (later retimed 10.44 pm) Brighton-Steyning daily. This non- standard timing was for the benefit of theatre-goers at Brighton and to make a connection off the 9.28 pm Victoria-Brighton/West Worthing.

After the push-and-pull working ended, extra coupling and uncoupling was, of course, necessary, and the following gives you some idea of the 'running about' undertaken by staff at Steyning. The 10.44 pm returned empty to Brighton (an empty train set for the first down service was detached at Steyning from a train of empties which ran on Monday

The loco is propelling this Horsham-Brighton train at Steyning in January 1960, so it has been necessary to push the train past the platform and water column to enable the engine to stand alongside the column. *D. V. Morgan*

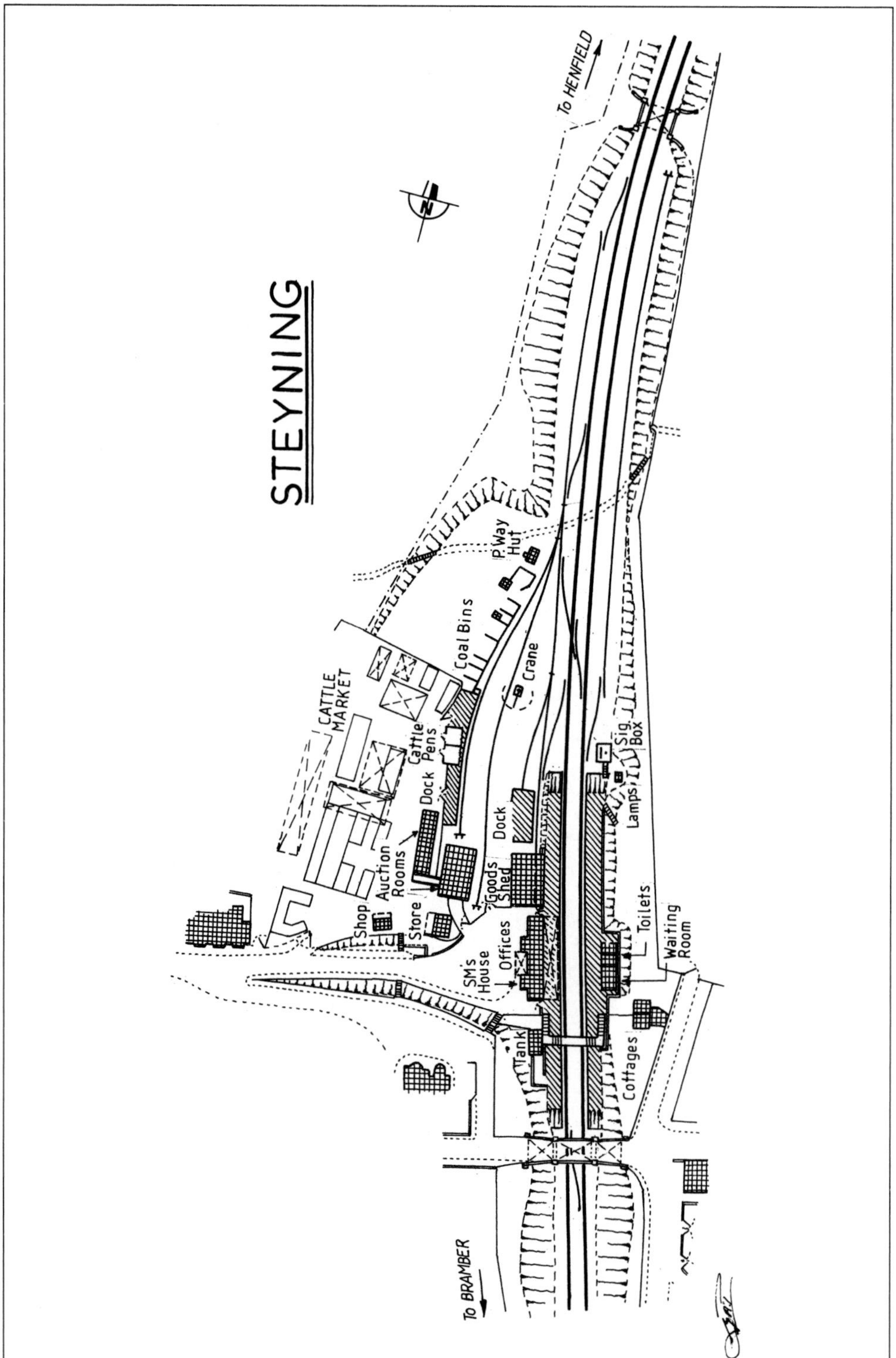

Steyning station plan. *George A. Pryer*

to Friday evenings from Horsham to Brighton, a van of market produce being attached to this train at Henfield).

When the last up train arrived at Steyning at night, the signalman would 'pull off' the starting signal and leave the box as soon as he received 'Train Entering Section' from Shoreham Bridge. He would then go down to the platform to collect the tickets and lock the station; also, when the train had stopped, he would go down to uncouple the engine, which would run forward clear of the north crossover. He would then walk back to the signal box and reset the crossover and ground signal for the driver to 'run round'. After the loco had run through the platform, the signalman would set the south crossover and again walk to the far end of the platform to recouple the engine, after having given the 'Is Line Clear?' signal and operated the signals. Returning to the box once more, he would give 'Train Entering Section' for the empty stock. Before receiving 'Train Out Of Section' from Shoreham Bridge, he told us that he had his key in the door, his motor cycling gear on, his cycle started and the pole hanging on the gas lamp chain for a quick getaway!

On Sunday nights the 10.44 pm Brighton-Steyning berthed in the yard, which meant that the staff at Steyning only had to sweep out the stock on Monday mornings, as on other days the set detached from the evening empty train was clean.

One morning we were rather amazed to see only two coaches in the siding, our staff having inadvertently split the train between coaches instead of between sets; so somewhere, someone had to locate four coaches and arrange a meeting!

As I mentioned earlier, the Worthing and District Growers Association sent produce from a number of stations to London markets and Bramber would load direct into the 7.14 pm SX Brighton-Horsham. Steyning would either load into the train or order a van in advance to load into, and attach it to this service. The problem had to be decided in advance whether the quantity would justify ordering a complete van or, on the other hand, would there be room in the train brake for the produce that we would be sending? We were in a 'no win' situation - the amount of time taken in detaching the train engine, reversing into the yard to collect the van and returning to its train was about the same as that taken by loading off the platform. The signalman usually helped with the loading - as did some of the passengers! The train was booked at Steyning for 8 minutes in any case. In addition, quite a few barrows were needed and plenty of covered space away from hot sun, rain or cold wind.

Each station except Bramber had a signal box and, as I have mentioned, Steyning was switched in virtually all day, the others being switched in and out as dictated by the traffic. In later years only Steyning, Beeding Sidings and Southwater boxes remained. The latter was used in connection with 'double block' working during fog and snow, otherwise Itchingfield Junction would not be able to accept a train from Steyning, say, until the signalman there had the points set for it over the junction; the resulting delay to the Mid Sussex service would be colossal! On a Sunday Steyning and Henfield would switch in for a van train of market produce, and if an excursion train was running (as we had from time to time from Reading to Brighton) boxes would switch in and out to split up the sections. It was difficult to arrange in advance which boxes were best suited for this as a little late running could upset the plans and cause delay to the traffic. These excursions ran via Horsham to reverse and were usually hauled by a 'Q' or 'Q1' Class loco. As I have said, staff became very versatile as they then had to work in office, signal box and platform at the same time, and most did this reasonably well. Partridge Green box was just outside the booking hall door and so was ideally situated for switching in for emergencies, especially in view of the fact that it was roughly halfway along the line. The others were at the far end of the platforms, so a long walk by staff was necessary.

Most summers a 'ramblers' excursion ran. This was arranged by a London organisation who would fill a special train almost every Sunday with their members, spending the Sabbath hiking and visiting a different venue every time. Bramber sported the longest platform on the branch, only half being tarred and lit, but at least the 'ramblers' did not have to 'pull up' there.

The Steyning line also provided an ideal alternative route from London to Brighton. Freight trains were often diverted at night up or down but timings were such that no intermediate signal boxes had to be switched in, the section being Shoreham Bridge to Itchingfield Junction, some 16 miles. The only fatality occurred on the line when an up freight diversion collided with a down freight at Itchingfield Junction when the latter was running on to the Mid Sussex line. The Type 3 Crompton diesel-electric locos were in use then and one thought which was put forward was that the driver was either overcome by fumes or went to sleep. This was the first diesel loco of what became Class 33 to be scrapped. Another stir of excitement was caused one morning when the 11.30 am Brighton-Plymouth ran via Steyning and reversed at Horsham due to a derailment at Lancing.

Livestock was quite frequently forwarded and received by stations on the branch, and West Grinstead dealt with horseboxes on a

Monday/Tuesday to Friday/Saturday,
19th/20th to 23rd/24th October, inclusive—continued

126—*contd.*—**ENGINEER'S WORKS.**—*continued.*

<table>
<tr><th>TIME</th><th>FROM</th><th>TO</th><th>ALTERATIONS.</th></tr>
<tr><td>Tues. to Sat.
a.m.</td><td></td><td></td><td></td></tr>
<tr><td>12 30Q ...</td><td>Waddon Marsh ...</td><td>Norwood Yard ...</td><td>Timing not available.</td></tr>
<tr><td>12 35 ...</td><td>Three Bridges ...</td><td>Redhill ... ...</td><td>Retimed:—Redhill Stn. 1.0-1.23 a.m., Redhill Down Yard arrive 1.28 a.m.</td></tr>
<tr><td>12||37 ...</td><td>Forest Hill ... ..</td><td>Bricklayers A. Shed</td><td>Additional Light Engine after banking 12.10 a.m., Bricklayers Arms.</td></tr>
<tr><td>12 45 ...</td><td>Lewes East Sidings ...</td><td>Bricklayers Arms</td><td rowspan="3">LL Coulsdon North to Norwood Yard.</td></tr>
<tr><td>1||52 ...</td><td>Horsham ... ...</td><td>Norwood Yard</td></tr>
<tr><td>3 45 ...</td><td>Horsham ... ...</td><td>Norwood Yard</td></tr>
<tr><td>1 10 ...</td><td>Redhill ... ...</td><td>Woking ... ...</td><td>Retimed.</td></tr>
<tr><td>1||30 ...</td><td>Brighton Shed ...</td><td>Preston Park ...</td><td>Additional light engine:—Brighton Shed depart 1||30 a.m., Brighton Stn. arrive 1||33 a.m. depart 1||35 a.m. Preston Park arrive 1||38 a.m. to work 1.30 a.m. Brighton from Preston Park to Hove.</td></tr>
<tr><td>1 30 ...</td><td>Brighton Top Yd. ...</td><td>Eastleigh ... ...</td><td>Retimed:—Preston Park arr. 1B35 a.m., dep. 1SH44 a.m. (TE to be provided) Hove arr. 1.52 a.m., dep. 2EL50B a.m.</td></tr>
<tr><td>1||45EL ...</td><td>Brighton Stn. ...</td><td>Preston Park ...</td><td>Additional light E.L. to work 10.32 p.m. Galley Hill from Preston Pk.</td></tr>
<tr><td>1 50 ...</td><td>Three Bridges ...</td><td>Battersea Yard ...</td><td>LL Coulsdon North to Windmill Bridge Jn.</td></tr>
<tr><td>2 0 ...</td><td>Three Bridges ...</td><td>Brighton ... ...</td><td>Retimed and diverted via Steyning.</td></tr>
<tr><td>2 25 ...</td><td>Redhill Up Yard ...</td><td>Hove ... ...</td><td>Retimed and diverted via Steyning.</td></tr>
<tr><td>2 30 ...</td><td>Willesden (L.M.R.)</td><td>Three Bridges ...</td><td>TL from South Croydon.</td></tr>
<tr><td>3 10EL ...</td><td>Lewes East Sidings ...</td><td>Norwood Yard ...</td><td>LL Coulsdon North to East Croydon ¶ to TL at East Croydon.</td></tr>
<tr><td>3 15 ...</td><td>Norwood Yard ...</td><td>Streatham ... ...</td><td>Will run via Chalk Section at Norwood Yard.</td></tr>
<tr><td>3 40 ...</td><td>Norwood Yard ...</td><td>Hove ... ...</td><td>Retimed, diverted via Steyning and extended to Brighton.
Formation from Norwood Yard:—
Engine, Hove traffic, brake van, Brighton traffic, brake van.</td></tr>
<tr><td>3 45 ...</td><td>Battersea Yard ...</td><td>Three Bridges ...</td><td>TL from South Croydon.</td></tr>
<tr><td>3 50 ...</td><td>Norwood Yard ...</td><td>Tattenham C. SX
Purley SO</td><td>Retimed:—South Croydon pass 4/1 a.m. and 2 minutes later to Purley.</td></tr>
<tr><td>3||56 ...</td><td>Brighton Shed ...</td><td>Hove ... ...</td><td>Retimed:—Brighton Shed depart 3||30 a.m., Brighton Stn. 3||33-3||35 a.m., Hove arrive 3||40 a.m.</td></tr>
<tr><td>4||10 ...</td><td>Hove ... ...</td><td>Brighton Shed ...</td><td>Retimed and diverted to Preston Park——Hove dep. 3||50 a.m. Preston Park arr. 3||55 a.m.
To work:—4.13 a.m. to Brighton Top Yard.</td></tr>
<tr><td>4 35Q ...</td><td>Moreton Cutting ...</td><td>Tonbridge ... ...</td><td>Will run B.</td></tr>
<tr><td>5 5 ..</td><td>Three Bridges ...</td><td>Brighton ... ...</td><td>Retimed.</td></tr>
<tr><td>5 55 ...</td><td>Preston Park ...</td><td>Brighton ... ...</td><td>Will not run.</td></tr>
</table>

<table>
<tr><th>Train ... ...</th><th colspan="2">12||37 a.m.
Forest Hill</th></tr>
<tr><td></td><td colspan="2">Tues. to Sat.
a.m.</td></tr>
<tr><td></td><td>arr.</td><td>dep.</td></tr>
<tr><td>Forest Hill ... ...</td><td>...</td><td>12||37</td></tr>
<tr><td>New Cross Gate ... ...</td><td>12</td><td>44</td></tr>
<tr><td>Bricklayera Arms Jn. ...</td><td>12</td><td>46</td></tr>
<tr><td>Bricklayers Arms NKW. ...</td><td>12||54</td><td></td></tr>
</table>

Monday/Tuesday to Friday/Saturday, 19th/20th to 23rd/24th October, inclusive—continued

126—*contd.*—ENGINEER'S WORKS.—*continued.*

Train	2.0 a.m. Three Bridges.		2.25 a.m. Redhill.		3.40 a.m. Norwood Yard.		5.5 a.m. Three Bridges	
	Tues. to Sat. a.m.		Tues. to Sat. a.m.		Tues. to Sat. a.m.		Tues. to Sat. a.m.	
	arr.	dep.	arr.	dep.	arr.	dep.	arr.	dep.
Three Bridges Yard ...	...	2 5	2B53	3 35	...	...	...	...
Three Bridges Station ...	2 10	2 13	3 40	3 42	4B36	4 38	...	...
Horsham Station	2L39	2L40	4L 7	4L 8	5L 3	5L 4	...	...
Itchingfield Jn.	2	48	4	16	5	12	...	...
Steyning	3	30	4	51	5	45	...	...
Shoreham-by-Sea	3	40	5	6	6	1	...	...
Hove	3	55	5 20	...	6 12	6 30	...	...
Haywards Heath	...	...	...	...	...	...	...	...
Keymer Jn.	...	...	...	...	...	...	...	...
Burgess Hill	...	...	...	...	...	...	...	...
Hassocks	...	...	...	...	...	...	6B10	6 53
Preston Park	4 3 T	E 4 13	...	...	6 38	6 47	7	6
Brighton Top Yard ...	4 20	...	...	...	6 52	...	7 11	...

Train	3‖15 a.m. Redhill Shed	
	Tues. to Fri. a.m.	
	arr.	dep.
Redhill Stn.	3‖17	3‖18
Edenbridge...	3	38
Tonbridge West Yard ...	3‖57	...

Train	12.15 p.m. Moreton Cutting W.R.		7‖12 p.m. Redhill Shed		3.25 p.m. Moreton Cutting W.R.		7.4 p.m. Reading South		10‖34 p.m. Redhill Shed		9.40 p.m. Reading South	
	Mon. to Fri. p.m.		Mon. to Fri. p.m.		Mon. to Fri. p.m.		Mon. to Fri. p.m.		Mon. to Fri. p.m.		Mon. to Fri. p.m.	
	arr.	dep.	arr.	dep.	arr.	dep.	arr.	dep.	arr.	dep.	arr.	dep.
Reading Spur	K	2 10	...	...	K	5 15	...	...	...	...	...	8 3
Reading South	...	...	...	...	...	...	...	7 4	...	...	...	...
Guildford ...	3	33	...	...	7	0	8 27	9 2	...	...	9	21
Shalford ...	3 53	6 8	...	...	7	8	9W14	9W19	...	...	9F30	9F43
Dorking Town	6	44	...	...	7	40	9	51	...	...	10	17
Betchworth	...	...	...	...	...	...	...	...	...	...	10F24	10F39
Reigate ...	7	0	...	...	8	0	10	5	...	...	10	48
Redhill Up Yd.	...	...	...	...	...	...	10 15	...	...	...	11 0	12 9 a.m.
Redhill Stn. ...	7L9	7L10	7‖15	7‖20	8L9	8L15	...	...	10	36	...	...
Merstham ...	7 20	11 7	7‖29	...	...	...	...	...	10‖41	...	...	...
Redhill Stn. ...	11	16	...	...	...	...	...	...	...	...	...	...
Redhill Down Yard	11 18	2 40 a.m.	...	...	...	...	...	...	...	...	12 13	...
Edenbridge ...	3	4	...	...	8	42	...	...	...	...	...	...
Tonbridge ...	3 27	...	...	...	9 9	...	...	...	...	...	...	...

K—Brake Van to be provided each end.

Left and above Extract from the Special Traffic Arrangements book for October 1959. This book was published weekly and showed alterations to the service due to sporting fixtures, engineering work, etc. The entries seen here show freight trains diverted from the main Brighton line to run via Steyning. The times 'spread over' the arrival and departure columns indicate passing times.

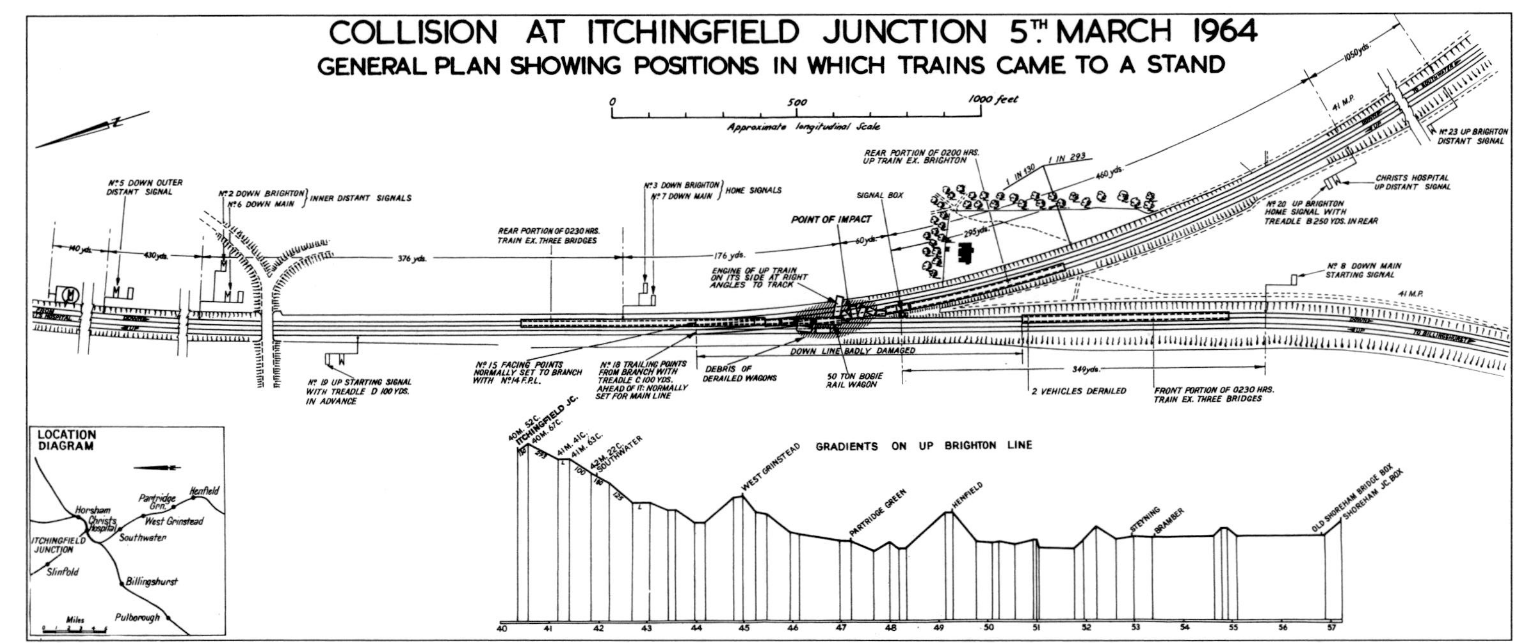

The map from the Ministry of Transport report into the 1964 accident at Itchingfield Junction. It also features a useful gradient profile of the Steyning line. *HMSO*

Type 3 Bo-Bo No D6502 was cut up on site following the Itchingfield Junction collision. ***John Scrace***

large scale, attaching them to or detaching them from passenger trains, the signal box, of course being switched in for this. The layout at West Grinstead made this easy as points did not have to be clipped or plugged since track circuits were provided there. When it was Findon Sheep Fair, a train of cattle trucks would be shunted into Steyning yard with an engine and brake van and crew standing by in case livestock was offered. On the last year that this took place, an epidemic of foot-and-mouth disease broke out and we had to refuse all the traffic and dispose of the empty wagons. Rather an expensive operation. Horseboxes were a type of wagon suitable for one or two horses with a compartment for the attendant who was able to lift a flap to feed the animal and keep an eye on it during transit. An attendant did not always travel with a horse - it must surely have been a slow, smelly and tedious journey!

I was called to Henfield one day when a couple of horses were offered for transit. The sender had given us the required advance notice and we obtained the 'service' from our Special Traffic Section. As a result we ordered a horse box and everyone was advised to which train the vehicle would be attached. The Senior Porter on duty thought that one horse looked unwell after the sender had left, so the arrangements had to be cancelled. What could we do? We could not risk sending a sick horse, but we could not take him out as there was nowhere to put him whilst the other went on his way. The question of feeding and bedding down would then arise. As we were completely ignorant about such matters, we called the local vet, who agreed that the animal should not travel. Eventually we obtained a second horse box and got rid of the 'good' horse and, after much persuasion, the sender eventually took the sick horse back after the railway's solicitor and vet had given him 'suitable advice'. We never knew for sure if the sender had planned it all or if it was purely a coincidence, but we were anxious to prevent a large claim had the animal died whilst in our custody.

From time to time livestock travelled 'on

foot' by passenger train. Sometimes it would be a dog on a lead or more often a calf, goat or ram which had to be 'persuaded' to board the train, much to the objection of the guard who usually found that the animal had eaten his sandwiches and made an unpleasant smell into the bargain! Rams and goats are known to be stubborn and, if they decided not to move, nothing would shift them. On the other hand they might prefer to be mobile, and one day when we had a ram to load 'passenger', we thought it was firmly tethered to the side of the goods shed wall - but we were wrong. The next time we saw it, it was in the churchyard and we had to call on the local farmers to catch it for us!

I came into the office one morning only to find that we had had burglars in the night; we slept immediately above but had heard nothing. Fortunately only the outer office had been entered and tickets and money were safe, although a few parcels had been opened and some of the staff's personal effects stolen. When the police questioned the 'late turn' staff asking about passengers coming off the last train the night before, one leading porter who had lived there all his life said 'There was a passenger alighted from the last train who was a stranger to me'!

My dealing with 'the law' became more numerous when lads were found to be tampering with the rolling-stock berthed in the yard, and also in connection with ticket irregularities, and when a lady passenger hit a member of the staff with her handbag! On these occasions I had to go to court as a witness and repeat the words used!

Speaking of ticket irregularities, I was always on the look out for season ticket holders who did not renew their tickets regularly. At a small station the staff knew a large proportion of the regular passengers, and if they did not renew their seasons they were missed. It was, of course, always possible that the new season could have been bought at the London end, or another possibility was that they had 'doctored' their seasons and extended the validity illegally. A passenger who had done that was 'ever so sorry' when I told him that I would have to report it. He eventually appeared at the local court and got a heavy fine.

The smaller the station the more intimately one knows the passengers, and I remember a day when the service was running very late and a lady who lived nearby suggested that she return home for a few minutes instead of waiting on the platform. However, as the train was drawn by a Crompton Class 33, it made up time out of all reason and we had to send a member of staff to the lady's house to fetch her as it was then almost right time. Another way to get the service back to time was to terminate a train from Horsham at Shoreham-by-Sea and restart the next service from there.

Our 'omnibus' telephone circuit was poor to say the least. Any member of staff at any station on the line could pick up the receiver and listen to a conversation, if the line was not too noisy. The station being called was summoned by a special code ring and, as you can imagine, the other stations would wonder why such and such a station was being called and would listen in. The GPO or 'National' telephone became used more and more as the BR circuits deteriorated which were also, of course, no good for confidential calls.

Staff would play pranks on other stations by posing as a passenger and ringing up another station on the GPO circuit to ask outlandish questions such as sending a motor cycle to Ireland or something similar. Suspecting that it might be another station, but unsure whether or not it was, the receiving station would give a short buzz on the railway circuit and, if the sound was heard through the telephone, the victim could be sure that the call was originating at a booking office, and give a suitable answer to the enquiry!

Each station has its own local personalities and Steyning was no exception. A lady whom we knew quite well was retired and travelled frequently, taking her very old father, who was totally deaf, out in his bath chair, then returning home for another old lady, also in a wheel chair; she then duly took them both by train to Brighton or some nearby station. I admired her courage when she took them both by train to the Chelsea

Flower Show. While she was returning for the old lady we would try and have a conversation with her deaf father, but this was difficult as the only hearing aid he had was an old-fashioned ear trumpet. He would try and buy the tickets, but as he spoke softly into his beard we invariably gave him the wrong thing. On one occasion we sold him tickets to Huddersfield instead of Wivelsfield, and he almost paid for them, remarking 'It is a bit dear, isn't it?' He was well known in the local church as he enjoyed hymn-singing, but as he could not hear the organ the other worshippers had to wait for him to stop singing to continue the service.

His daughter was always trying to think of somewhere new to take him and was toying with the idea of a day trip to France. I pointed out that (then) a passport-size photograph was required for each person. She said this was no problem, and reappeared with a picture taken about 50 years earlier of a dapper, debonair young man. I said that a recent look-alike was required, but she said that this was her father when he worked for the Water Board! I never found out if the French trip came about but, knowing her, it probably did.

Fortunately celebrities are allowed to come and go as they please in their own town without crowds and without fingers being pointed. Amongst our passengers were the lovable music hall couple Elsie and Doris Waters ('Gert & Daisy') and we also had frequent visits from a BBC producer who had come to live there. He was a charming man and always visited the station on his moped. On one occasion he was expecting a carpet by rail and I often wondered how he would convey it home as he himself more than filled the bike with his large frame!

My association with another TV character was not quite so happy. I had cause to ring this man to discuss a claim for a damaged parcel and I cannot say I actually spoke to him as he told me my fortune, what he thought of BR, and what he thought of my ancestors in no uncertain terms!

Dealing with claims, etc, was never one of my favourite pastimes, and one day a perambulator arrived by train looking like a tangle of barbed wire, having fallen from the platform in front of an electric train at Horsham. I decided that the fairest way would not be to offer the pram by the delivery motor but walk round to the lady's house and explain the circumstances. The lady who came to the door looked as though she would need the pram very shortly, so I decided against saying 'I have bad news for you' or 'There has been an accident' as my first aid knowledge may have been necessary there and then! To cut a long story short the lady was very understanding and I told her to write in and claim.

Working for a concern such as BR with staff scattered across the map, there is little time or the opportunity for socialising, but we ran a first aid class at Steyning in a room above the local Railway Hotel to which one or two staff from each station came. Of course, one 'gang' could never come as they were at work. Our team members were made up of Head Office staff, permanent way men and staff from nearby stations; we would have lectures from a local doctor and very much enjoyed entering very realistic competitions against teams from other stations. Even in later years I continued to keep up my first aid training and we even went away for a weekend some time later for combined meal, social evening and competition.

If I was travelling to visit another station I would often travel in the guard's van as I knew most of the crews, and some journeys still remain in my mind. A Horsham driver received a commendation for pulling up his train suddenly to avoid hitting hounds when the hunt was crossing the track. It would have been expensive to replace such valuable animals and the Master of Foxhounds wrote in to thank the driver.

Some of the instances which I have related demonstrate the ruralness of the line, as does my next story. A trainee driver was on the footplate one day with his instructor and between stations a lovely field of mushrooms came into view. He requested his mate to drop him off to pick a few, suggesting that he could be picked up on the next trip. By chance I returned with the same crew and they had great difficulty in remembering exactly where they had left the other driver,

(Form referred to in Rule 183, clause (f)). B.R. 87212

BRITISH RAILWAYS

.... Region

A supply of these Forms must be kept by each Guard.

WRONG LINE ORDER FORM
GUARD TO SIGNALMAN **A**

To the Signalman at .... signal box

Allow an engine, an engine and vehicles, or breakdown van train to travel in the wrong direction to my train which is stationary on the *.............. line at ....

I will prevent my train being moved until the engine, engine and vehicles, or breakdown van train arrives.

Catch points, spring or unworked trailing points exist at ....

Signed........................Guard.

Date .... 19.......... Time issued ....m.

†Countersigned........................
Driver of engine assisting in rear.

† Countersigned ....
Signalman
at .... signal box

* Insert name of line, for example, Up or Down Main, Fast, Slow or Goods.

† If necessary.

'Wrong Line Order Forms' were used by driver, guard or signalman to authorise a wrong direction movement in an emergency. For example, a driver might request an assisting engine to come back on to his train, but only after a full understanding had been reached by all concerned.

as one field looked much like another. He was wondering how he could go in to his depot at Brighton and say 'I lost my mate somewhere along the line' - but then how long could he keep the train whilst he searched? The driver decided to carry on to the next station, where happily the other driver was waiting after having walked along the track. What a relief!

We had our usual crop of engine failures, particularly with 'M7s', but some of the other causes of delay to trains were typically 'country', the sort of thing which could not happen in a suburban area. I well remember the first up train one Sunday running into a herd of cattle which had got through an open gate. Cows are large animals and several members of the track staff had to take away by trolley parts of these heavy animals which were trapped under the train. We had a couple of derailments too. The first, less serious, happened when our Porter Signalman was bringing the rolling-stock for the 7.35 am out of the yard; he signalled the driver to reverse too far, knocked the stop blocks off and almost put the coaches down the bank.

The second occasion was on the main line and involved the 'evening empties', causing single line working to be introduced between Steyning and Henfield for the remainder of the evening. At some small stations not every move had a ground signal provided for it, and on the evening in question, when detaching our 'three set' to berth in the down siding, the signalman operated the siding points but failed to notice a flint between the blades and the first coach became derailed.

I got to know many of the schoolboys and some of the masters quite well (sometimes through the former's misbehaviour). They did some research and found that the Steyning line was 100 years old and wondered what could be done to celebrate it. There were various 'railway groups' who often brought me snippets of information which they had researched, and I was interested in it but with the short time available, so few people interested and no money, I could see no way in which anything could be done. The boys found old press cuttings and I went to the Grammar School and listened to tapes which they had made about their research - again I was not optimistic until one evening there was a knock at my door and a stranger introduced himself as Bernard Holden, who was then head of the Train Running Section at our Divisional Office at Croydon, and he offered to help. (He is currently writing a history of the Steyning line, and has also been closely associated with the progress of the preserved Bluebell Line in many ways.) Between us we arranged to celebrate the centenary of the opening of the north end of the line on Saturday 7 October 1961. (The south end of the line was opened on 1 July 1861, but time was too short to celebrate that date.)

BR's Publicity Office at Waterloo arranged an exhibition in the waiting room at Steyning and a special print of tickets was made for a round trip on the branch on the date in question. The station was dressed in

The special excursion train marking the centenary of the Steyning branch arrives at Steyning station. Large crowds gathered, a special souvenir ticket was issued, and radio and television recorded the event. The loco, 0-6-2T No 32468, was polished and ran with the special headboard all day. *Shoreham Herald*

STEYNING
BRANCH
CENTENARY
1961
32468

LOCOMOTIVE
No 32635
STEYNING

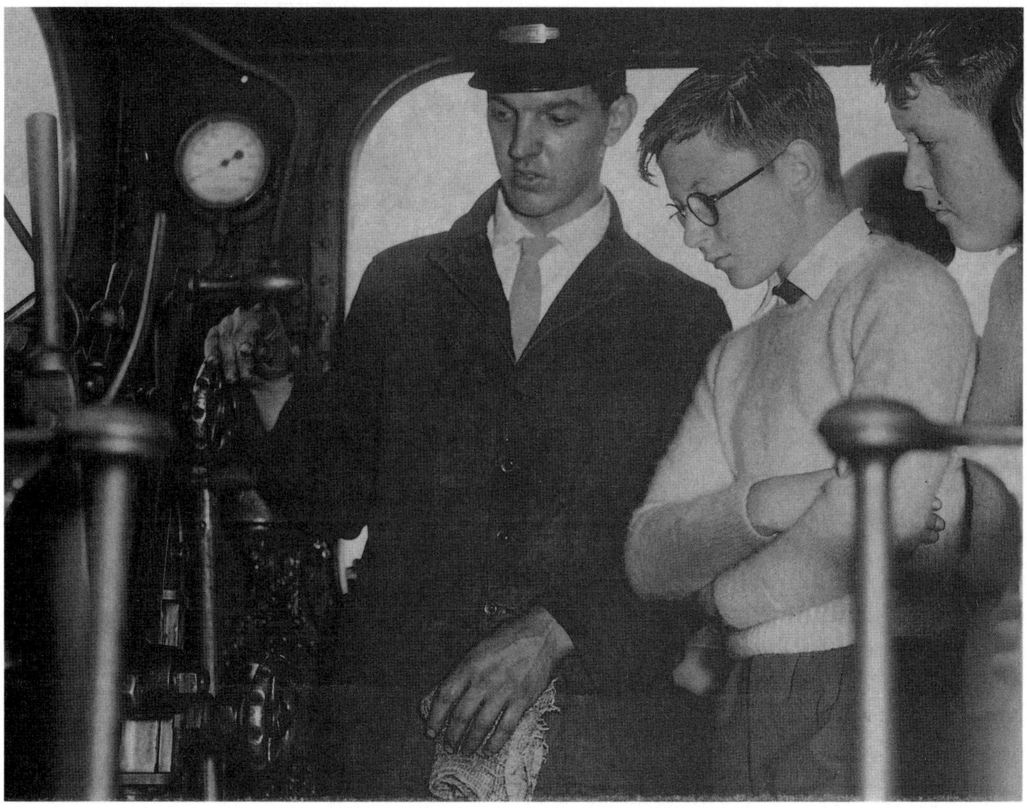

In the cab of No 32635. ***Shoreham Herald***

bunting and the Brighton Works shunting engine, 'A1X' 0-6-0T No 32635, was on show in the yard. A special headboard was carried on 'E4' 0-6-2T No 32468 which hauled a number of the trains on that day. It was in immaculate condition and the BR management went to a lot of trouble for us.

As far as I am aware nothing had been done like this before, but in later years Open Days such as those at Ashford and Brighton were becoming commonplace.

My wife Mary and a local cafe owner, Betty Searle, served refreshments from the house. Local radio and TV covered the event

Above left **Another view of the centenary celebrations.** ***Author***

Left **The Brighton Works shunter, 0-6-0T No 32635, on display at Steyning. The station and signal box were decked with flags and an exhibition was arranged in the waiting room.** ***Shoreham Herald***

but we were unable to see it as we were outside the area to receive it. A very enjoyable day was had by all.

On several occasions I have been present when radio and TV interviews take place and, at one such interview, I approached the well-known interviewer and asked him for an autograph, which he gladly gave. I could not catch his name, nor could I read it and, as I never heard the interview in question, I eventually discarded my treasured autograph and made a mental note to write the name of the celebrity down should the occasion again arise!

Happily, the future of the line looked assured, as a plan for electrification was in the offing. The Area Inspector had walked the track to check on positions for sub stations and to ensure that there would be no problems with conductor rails over bridges, foot crossings, etc. A weekend of single line

Centenary of the Horsham-Shoreham Railway 29.6.61

ON July 1, 1861, after years of discussion, contention and frustration, the first official train ran up the line from Shoreham to Partridge Green.

A branch line from Shoreham to serve the countryside around Steyning and Henfield was first projected as early as 1845, and two years later the Brighton and South Coast Railway Co. actually raised the money to build the line, but at the last moment decided to spend it elsewhere.

Nearly ten years passed before the question of the line was raised again, but at long last, in 1857, the necessary Bill was laid before Parliament. However, the route of the line did not satisfy local landowners and they decided to fight the B.S.C. Railway. Headed by Percy Burrell, of Knepp Castle, the Rev. John Goring, of Wiston, and Hugh Ingram, of Steyning, they decided to promote their own company for the same purpose, and a bitter battle began between the rival bodies.

Shoreham, Horsham and Dorking Railway Co., as it was called, proceeded to place its own Bill before Parliament, and both Bills obtained their second reading in February, 1858. Then came a blow for the landowners. The Wimbledon-Dorking Co. and the Epsom-Leatherhead Railway, with which the Shoreham line was to connect, refused to amalgamate, and this substantially reduced the possibilities of the new line.

RIVAL COMPANIES

In April both Bills went before a Committee of the House of Commons, and for nine days the merits of the rival companies were fiercely debated and minutely examined. At last the decision was given. The landowners' scheme was turned down, and their defeat left the way clear for their rivals to obtain an unopposed passage of their Bill in the House of Lords.

With victory in their hands, the B.S.C. Railway pressed forward with their plans, and in August, 1858, with great rejoicing, the first sod of the new railway was cut and work began all along the route.

Although there were to be comparatively few cuttings, five bridges had to be constructed and there were many other difficulties. The greatest obstacle was the marsh beyond Steyning known as Bokeney Bog. For three months 500 loads of chalk were brought up each day by the operational trucks and dumped into the marsh. At one time the engineer feared that the task would prove too difficult, but finally the bog was conquered and the line turned towards Henfield. One change was made in the route, and the line was to go to Southwater instead of Itchingfield as originally planned.

For many months work proceeded at a leisurely pace and the inhabitants of Henfield and Steyning complained bitterly about the delay. At last the company decided that part of the line, as far as Partridge Green, could be opened for a start, and in June, 1861, the Government Inspector came to examine the line. The station buildings were not finished, but wooden huts were erected for the sale of tickets, and although only a single line had been laid, a double track was to be completed when the other stations were opened.

TESTING THE BRIDGES

The engineer, Mr. G. Hawker, and Mr. Joseph Firbank, the contractor, were among those present. Four heavy locomotives were used and they were see-sawed to and fro over all the bridges to test their strength. When a thorough examination had been made, the whole party went back to Steyning and enjoyed an excellent dinner at the White Horse Hotel. The inspection proved perfectly satisfactory and accordingly it was decided formally to open the line on Monday, July 1.

On that morning a preliminary train ran up the line depositing the station masters and stores at their respective stations. The news that at last Puffing Billy was really on the move spead quickly through the countryside, and the people, some of whom had probably never seen a train before, turned out in their masses to, "witness the wonder of the age."

The official opening train was the 1.50 p.m. from Brighton, and this carried a large number of passengers and officials. When they reached Shoreham, the engine was decorated with flags, while the Storrington 8th Sussex Rifle Band began to play. At Steyning the whole town was gathered at the station, flags flying, church bells ringing, and as the train drew in the band struck up "God Save the Queen." A vast number of people got in the train and away they went to Henfield, where a similar demonstration took place, and more passengers were taken on for the last stage to Partridge Green. On arrival the passengers got out, the band struck up again and continued to play until it was time for the return journey to Steyning. Here nearly the whole company left the train, and headed by the band, marched in procession up the decorated road.

DINNER AT STEYNING

The inhabitants of Steyning, with great liberality, gave a dinner for the visitors, provided by Mr. Steele at the White Horse, with enormous success —"the viands being all that could be desired, the champagne and other wines of excellent vintage and the dessert choice and pleasing." Nearly 100 gentlemen sat down under the presidency of the Rev. George Airey of Steyning, and many toasts were drunk, speeches made and the company entertained with songs and music.

At last the procession formed up once more, and followed by an enthusiastic crowd of Steyning people, marched back to the station and entrained for Brighton.

From July onwards three trains ran daily in each direction, with frequent special excursions to the Crystal Palace (3s. 6d. return) and Portsmouth (2s. return).

Work on the line proceeded apace, and was almost complete when disaster came to the Brighton Railway with the Clayton Tunnel accident on Sunday, August 25, 1861. On that morning the Portsmouth excursion went into the tunnel followed soon after by the Brighton express. But the special signalling arrangements failed, and the train in the tunnel started to back out. Unfortunately the following train had just gone through the entrance and a dreadful collision occurred. Twenty-two passengers lost their lives and many were injured, while the appalling scenes in the darkness of the tunnel shocked and horrified the whole nation.

Thus it was that the second part of the railway, from Partridge Green, through West Grinstead and Southwater to Horsham, was opened for traffic on September 16 without the slightest publicity.

MARGARET HOLT

A newspaper cutting recounting the opening of the Steyning line in 1861.

working between Steyning and Beeding was arranged but had to be cancelled due to excessively bad weather. On another weekend, when the new A24 bridge was being put in between Horsham and Christ's Hospital, a diesel multiple unit service was used between Brighton and the latter point to save 'running round' moves, and the DEMUs took over permanently on 4 May 1964, sometimes using 'Oxted' units but more often 'Hampshire' units. We found the brake van accommodation too small for all the prams on a Saturday afternoon; one of the compartments was later adapted for luggage but with only a single door the exercise was rather pointless. The timetable was accelerated and a considerable economy made. The stations were kept cleaner and our wives were especially pleased as they could put washing on the clothes line and, for the first time, not find it covered with smuts.

Steyning was the only station on the branch with '3-car' and '6-car' stop signs, as the first up train on Monday to Fridays was formed of two units, one being detached to form our 07.35 to Brighton.

I was still at Steyning when the Beeching Report came out, but as almost every secondary route in the country was included we did not seriously consider closure. Objections were put before the Transport Users Consultative Committee, and closure was delayed until a meeting was held at Steyning. The meeting was well attended and gave BR a 'rough ride'. Strangely enough the last thing BR wanted to do was to lose an alternative route, and the existing service was left in force until final closure on 7 March 1966. A lot of 'red herrings' were put up by the objectors such as livestock and market produce which were, by then, a thing of the past. I always felt that it was very unfair that a small, little-used station might survive because it was on a main line, but a reasonably used one on a branch line surrounded by other poorly used stations was doomed.

9.
FARNINGHAM ROAD AND BECKENHAM 1964-70
From Station Master to Clerical Instructor

The actual closure of Steyning took place after I moved away, because in 1964 I was promoted to station master at Farningham Road, between Swanley and Rochester. When I went there I was surprised to find the goods yard still in use, as many had closed by then. We were still receiving coal and a few other 'full loads' and it was rumoured that a large steel works was to be erected there on the many acres of spare land which was available on the 'up' side. Here could be seen several sidings long since abandoned and now overgrown. (The steelworks were opened a few years later and for a while had rail access).

Farningham Road box was switched in when a freight went in or out of the yard or a train was being sent down the single goods line to Gravesend West. The box had a small panel which operated the junction where previously Fawkham Junction box had been. This branch was operated as 'one train working' with a 'dead' staff with a key on the end for intermediate sidings; the staff was not

'R1' Class 0-4-4T No 31660 at 'Farningham Road and Sutton-at-Hone', to give the station its full name, with a Gravesend train. *Real Photographs*

An earlier view, in Southern days, of an 'R1' having arrived at Gravesend West Street (in later years the word 'Street' was dropped from the station title. In any case it was in the north of Gravesend.) *Real Photographs*

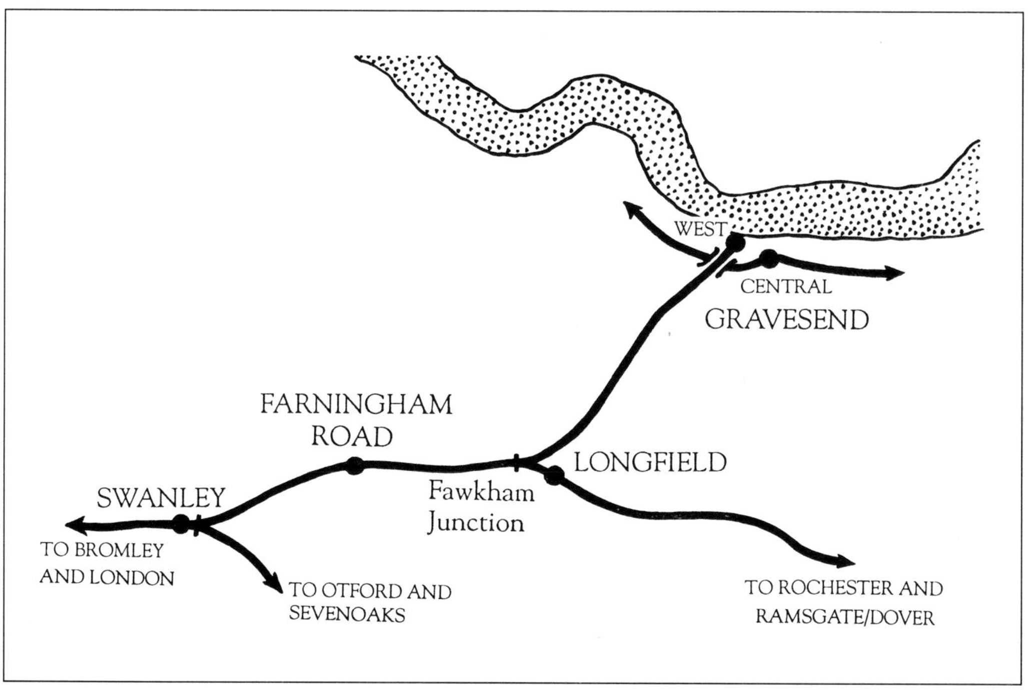

Lines around Farningham Road. *Christina Siviter*

My daughter Rosalind assisting with 'parcels' rated traffic at Farningham Road. Animals sent 'on foot' were not uncommon, but were not popular with guards for obvious reasons. ***Author***

issued from a tablet machine at Farningham Road. The main-line signalling was 'track circuit block' and the signals were semi-automatic, in other words when Farningham Road switched out, the signals returned to automatic working. The box at Longfield was only used once or twice a year when engineering work made it necessary.

The main line through Farningham Road was a renowned spot for fast running and before I came and after I left there were several derailments of freight trains there, train ferry wagons usually being responsible. It was said that several fruit trees had grown up along the line as a result of fruit spilled when a wagon turned over! I am reminded of the time when a 'ferry van' arrived at Farningham Road from the continent for a local consignee and our attention was drawn to an important notice on the outside of the van in a foreign language which, of course,

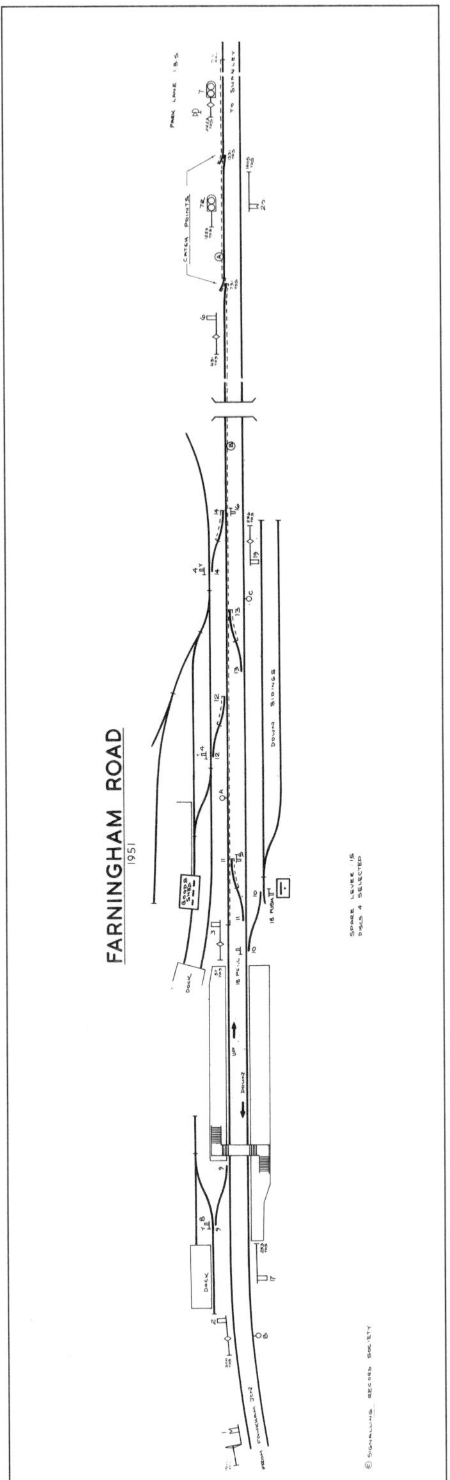

The track and signalling layout at Farningham Road in 1951, when Fawkham Junction signal box was still open. *Signalling Record Society*

HARTLEY AND ASH
RURAL PRESERVATION COMMITTEE

Public Demonstration

at 7.30 a.m.

Longfield Station

TO SIMULATE CONDITIONS WHICH ARE LIKELY TO EXIST IF THE NEW TOWN IS BUILT NEAR HARTLEY

Come to the station, if possible by car, and attempt to board the **7.41 a.m. train** or the **8.09 a.m. train**

Television, Radio, the National and Local Press will be there to report the event

---

WE WANT THE STATION AND ITS APPROACHES CROWDED TO CAPACITY

Tuesday 1st June, 1965

ORDERLY BEHAVIOUR IS ESSENTIAL
COME EARLY IN CASE YOU MISS IT
YOUR SUPPORT IS ESSENTIAL

I wonder how many people who now live in New Ash Green took part in this demonstration. Longfield has been used by a large number of commuters for many years.

we did not understand. Without further ado we opened the wagon door and were bombarded with loose oranges.

Both stations (Farningham Road and Longfield) presented problems with ticket checks as each had a footbridge away from the station buildings and it was impossible for one man to cover both. Both stations had a comparatively small off-peak usage but Longfield had an enormous number of commuters, and when the village at New Ash Green was under consideration, a demonstration was organised by local residents to show how public services would be stretched to saturation point; on the day in question hundreds of passengers packed on to the platform to such a degree that the ticket office at Longfield ran out of platform tickets. Radio and TV covered the demonstration and all parties considered the day a great success.

The off-peak service was hourly (between Victoria and Sheerness), operated by HAP units, and there was an hourly non-stopping service from and to Victoria-Ramsgate/Dover composed of CEP stock.

The station house which we occupied was small and compact, unlike most, but again the only piece of garden was on the other side of the track and when I had a bonfire there one afternoon I almost burned down the signal box! The house and signal box were lit by electricity but the station was gas lit. Farningham Road was a typical London, Chatham & Dover Railway station with very tiny buildings on one end of the platform. There was no structure on the down side except the underneath of an old water crane which served as a waiting room.

I was beginning to feel that a station master's life was not for me. I did not want to be continually moving nor to live in a railway house without a decent garden for my family; I also found 'on call' commitments a bit of a bugbear. Steyning had been somewhere apart and I never expected to find anywhere else to compare with it! In addition, the reduction in the number of goods yards, signal boxes and staff meant that the number of station masters/managers would greatly diminish or disapear altogether. Coupled to this, with improvements in 'outside' housing standards station houses were becoming less acceptable, and more and more SM's posts were advertised without a house. The station master's role as we knew it was changing completely. At about this time grades were being assimilated and, contrary to popular belief, an SM is not necessarily higher in grade than, say, a clerk. I knew of several people who took promotion only to find that they had gained nothing, either because their new post was abolished or their old one was upgraded. I had no visions of grandeur and would never want the worries which went with a large station. I therefore applied for a post as a Clerical Instructor at the Clerical Training School and was successful in being appointed.

It had always been my ambition to speak

in public but I was never able to do so. However, when I was successful in being appointed to the instructor's post at the Training School it was subject to passing an instructor's course at Darlington. Our first practice lecture was on any subject of our choice and each was recorded and played back whilst the other students politely asked questions and criticised. It is amazing how one is unaware of one's own habits and idiosyncrasies until they are pointed out.

One of the lads was ready to go home as he felt he had really 'fluffed' it, but strangely enough his tape recording was never found. I am sure that the instructors 'lost' his cassette through kindness, but all the students progressed well and passed with flying colours.

The weather was bitterly cold and snow almost covered the signposts in some areas. For a while the electricity was cut off and the lecturing was by candlelight. The purpose of the course was to teach one how to teach - our instructors assumed that we knew our subject. It mattered not whether the pupil was teaching woodwork, permanent way students, first aiders or any other subject, as the basic fundamentals were the same. I found it very useful and would have been terrified to stand up and speak to a class without their help and advice. They advocated that instructors should only teach for short periods before going back to their own work as one could get out of touch and lose enthusiasm. I had great difficulty in persuading our management that this was a good idea about five years later! I felt that after teaching office work over and over again I would make a very good clerk! I felt sorry for the students - I gave the course lessons over and over again and still learned more each time or saw things in a different light, whereas the students had to take it all in first time, and if a reasonable pass mark was not attained they were out.

Between courses we would make amendments to our books and update our instruction as changes were always being introduced. Amending one book is tedious enough, but by the time I had amended 15 or 16 books I was driven to distraction. At about this time cash registers were being introduced in ticket offices, so we held one-day courses for existing staff on this subject. Here we had to tread carefully as now we were dealing with experienced men and women from large stations, and all manner of problems would arise which trainees would not think of.

Cash registers dated and charged tickets, including seasons and paper tickets, accounted for them, something that the dating press did not do, and gave the clerk a figure for his shift to which he should balance his cash.

As I will explain later, all ticket offices are different. Several of us were called upon to work evenings and weekends in ticket offices which thus prevented us from getting 'rusty', but the resident staff at the stations we visited expected a very high standard from us! Sometimes at a station we would come across a new instruction which we had not seen and were able to update our instruction accordingly. On one or two occasions I was asked to supervise a station when engineering work was taking place at a weekend, to ensure that trains did not leave before the replacement buses had arrived, and vice versa. This was not always easy as, in a country area, buses were operating over roads not normally served by a direct bus, and some got lost!

During our courses for trainee clerks we sometimes went out and about to a large ticket office or station and sometimes to a location for fire-fighting instruction and for film shows. Another regular visit was to the Lost Property Office at Waterloo, which is the central 'pool' for all items found on the Southern Region. Here the problems were explained of coping with a Region's negligent passengers and the importance of adopting the correct procedures for items found, as sometimes legal action could be brought if an important item was opened when it should not have been, or time was wasted in reporting objects found, especially in the case of dangerous items. When at Hove I had a rifle and a few rounds of ammunition handed in, but in cases like that it is more likely that someone left it behind on purpose, as it was probably getting 'too hot'. I was always afraid that a pupil would embarrass me by asking an inane question and, sure enough, one day it happened. The manager of the Lost Property Office stated that everything found on the SR could be found here, to which a trainee asked 'Where do we find the hundred million pounds BR lost last year?'

Tracing lost property is always a chancy business and requires quite an element of luck. If one can call up another station whilst the train is en route, there is a fair chance of tracing the article, but once a period of time has elapsed the trail becomes cold, and the article could be travelling round in a train almost anywhere. Recently a passenger just could not believe that his wallet, containing about £1,000, was not handed in when he left it on a train. If only everyone was honest! It is particularly hard to determine the train in question if a passenger has changed at, say, London Bridge or East Croydon.

I was very amused one day when calling at a London Lost Property Office to be confronted by the attendant with a face full of shaving cream. Presumably he thought that there was time for a quick shave between customers and was caught out. Could you imagine that happening at a bank or post office?

Back at the classroom we gave instruction in commercial matters in the morning, and practical ticket office work in the afternoons. As return tickets were then two-part (to be torn in half), I pointed out the importance of reversing the routing on the return portion, eg 'via Dartford and Chatham' would ready 'via Chatham and Dartford' on the other portion, but this proved not always to be the case, as I pointed out to a pupil who was not conversant with the station name of Bat & Ball!

At first our school was housed in GLC offices but later at Waterloo and finally at Beckenham. At one of these places we got to know the contract cleaners quite well and one of them promised to get us some vacuum flasks cheaply. We said that we would all like one and eventually one appeared, but the cleaner was never seen again so we decided that the fairest thing would be to make a draw for it. As one member was sick we included his name and he won it; it then remained on the shelf until he returned. He was pleased to be told it was his but, on taking it home, he left it on the train and it was never seen again. I am sure there is a moral there!

In addition to clerical commercial courses we also conducted evening classes and a week's course of induction for new entrants, telling them about conditions of employment, pay, promotion prospects, welfare, etc, and included in this was a short talk by a retired railwayman about the Railway Home at Woking for children and old people to which contributions can be made direct through paybills. One day he was unable to come and I was asked to give the talk. As I walked out in front of the class, everyone was in fits of laughter. I did not know why, and checked my clothing and wondered if my breakfast was still on my face! I did not realise the reason until the other instructors told me afterwards that they had told the class to be very good as the speaker was a little deaf, very doddery and about 75 years old!

I found every course different. Some were good fun - others less so. In some cases a party followed the last day, and following some I was given a small present. In one case a reunion followed a year later. I still see quite a few of my old students at stations but I have difficulty in remembering names or who they were with.

10.
LONDON BRIDGE 1970-77, 90-92
In Control - 'British Rail regrets...'

When I was eventually released from the school I did temporary relief work again for a few months until going into a new post at London Bridge in about 1970. The management were anxious to set up a control point which would be manned round the clock, operate taped announcements and a short-wave radio, monitor the running of the service and advise the Divisional 'Control' of any late running, delays, etc. In addition to this, teleprinters were being installed, and London Bridge was one of the first; we therefore had to inform Charing Cross, Cannon Street and London Bridge signal boxes, station departments and 'out stations' of any cancellations, etc. A messenger was provided to take round information dealing with less important matters, such as stolen tickets, altered commercial practices, etc. At least here was a station at which I was working that was not likely to close!

I found the work very absorbing and there was not enough time to do everything required as one worked alone unless there

A wide view of the 'country end' of London Bridge station, South Eastern side. An up service stands at platform 6 on the left, while Class 415/1 EPBs Nos 5176/5185 leave platform 4 with an afternoon Sevenoaks service. The date is September 1982. ***Brian Morrison***

was a serious incident, when sometimes help was available. There were no such things as visual display units then and as the services in the evening and morning peaks were not at regular times or had standard stops, it was not easy to pick out which train was which, as we only had a repeater of the platform indicator which said, for example, 'Via Bexleyheath', and in a number of instances the timetable showed two trains with different stops on that route within a few minutes. To ensure that we knew which particular train was which, we listed the headcodes and formation (eg 4 + 2 EPB), whether it was First and Second Class or not, and any other information which would help to identify a train. I don't think we were often wrong!

You may think that someone announcing trains has little to do with a passenger tearing his clothes, but you are mistaken! Some late evening trains miss out certain stations and it was easy to use the wrong taped announcement. Apparently this happened late one evening when trains did not call at Woolwich Dockyard, and the operator used the 'all stations' tape. The driver, hearing this, thought he was required to do so. A passenger alighted at Woolwich Dockyard and, of course, could not get off the station as it is down low between two tunnels and surrounded by high walls. He tore his trousers while climbing the wall and claimed accordingly!

It is a strange sensation making announcements and wondering if anyone is listening. I was called upon to record some 'tapes' for station announcements and this seemed even more odd, to be sitting in an upstairs room over a shop in Croydon saying 'Hurry along please' or 'Stand away please - fast train passing'. When at London Bridge station my friends got very confused as they thought I was on duty when, in fact, I was not, as my voice was being heard on tape. As a result of this I was asked to record a commentary for a stand at the Boat Exhibition in London.

When a vacancy occurs anywhere, I suppose staff are anxious to know who their new mate is to be and where he lives. When we heard that a new operator was being appointed at London Bridge we asked the station master who he was, and he informed us that he was an Irishman who said that he lived at Yeovil. The SM agreed that he was the right man for the job, but doubted whether he could travel that distance for the turns of duty. We thought no more of it until he eventually arrived and we asked him where he lived. 'I live in London,' he said. 'The Oval at Kennington.'!

Naturally when our centre was first opened we were always being invaded by visitors both young and old. The SM brought some schoolchildren along one day to look round after they had listened to the taped announcements on the platform which were recorded by a woman. 'There you are,' he said. 'You see there is no lady here.' He was

Myself in the Control Point at London Bridge. It was constantly being photographed for various publications, including a book about computers, and was also featured on several radio and TV programmes.

The 'London' end of platform 6, with a Charing Cross to Tattenham Corner and Caterham train running in. The Control Point can be seen on the extreme right, and was built on the base of what had at one time been a signal box on the end of platforms 1 and 2. *Brian Morrison*

very apologetic afterwards when, out of his line of vision, the children caught sight of a female cleaner polishing the floor!

We also had visits by radio and TV reporters in connection with various events and Sir Richard Marsh, the then BR Chairman, paid a visit. On another occasion a Government minister was heard to remark 'Oh I did not realise that London Bridge was a station'!

It was some years later that the Duke of Edinburgh visited London Bridge on the occasion of the opening of the new signal box. His train consisted of a Class 33 'Crompton' diesel-electric locomotive and the General Manager's Saloon which glistened like new. The windows and brasswork were a sight to behold, but we searched in vain for our royal visitor - he was on the engine!

In the seven years that I was at London Bridge on the first occasion I saw many changes and dealt with many problems. We had major disruptions to the service due to cuts at a time of a power crisis, industrial actions by crews, long-term timetable alterations due to earthworks, bomb alerts and incidents, and, of course, the London Bridge resignalling and rebuilding programme. This was carried out in stages and there are numerous publications setting out how it came about. Cannon Street was closed for a few weeks in the summer of 1974 prior to the main 'changeover'; the service was temporarily altered to allow for this, and trains were diverted to and from Blackfriars, Charing Cross and Victoria, while some terminated at London Bridge. Our office had to be moved to alter relays, telephones and cables, and we were located in a small staff room under the stairs on platform 1. These various phases spanned several years and each brought a different batch of train service alterations and, of course, platforming changes connected with the rebuilding. Various lines were taken out of use at stages and brought back in again either with reversible running or for use in the opposite direction. Once it was all done the job was much easier as we had a VDU and each train was allocated a number which appeared on the screen; also other stations had teleprinters and much of our work disappeared. The short-wave radios were best suited to the terminal side of the station to locate a shunter or carriage examiner who could be anywhere on the station and not necessarily near a telephone, or when a member of staff had to go along the track for an emergency and reporting back was quicker by radio.

When we had Sunday engineering work we would often record a tape ourselves at home and use it at intervals to save the monotony of repeating the same message over and over again. This was usually all right, but when my daughter took a cassette to a party to listen to pop music they were rather put out when the first hit they heard was 'There is a special bus service from.....' Another member of our team made some tapes at home and, in the background, played his own recording of steam trains of the past, so passengers were seen to look in all directions for a steam engine at London Bridge whenever it was used! We were completely separate from the 'Central' side (the terminal platforms) which is out of sight due to the overall roof, but of course we maintained contact with them as terminating trains from the 'South Eastern' could be run into those platforms, as was the case during the big changeover to the new signalling when the eastern side was virtually closed for the whole Easter weekend in 1976.

The Central side is extremely busy in the peaks and one's work is taken up with watching many platforms as one platform change may mean trains being re-platformed for some while until the service gets back to normal again. The announcer on the Brighton side became involved in a court case when a passenger alleged that no announcement was made to the effect that certain stations beyond Worthing had short platforms and passengers had to join the front six coaches only to avoid being off the platform. The announcer had to announce the train in court and a member of the staff had to take along the 'finger' board which set out the part of the train to join. Such is the life of a railwayman.

I was grateful that I never had to announce the Eastbourne service via Oxted which had some considerable alliteration: East Croydon, Sanderstead, Riddlesdown, Upper Warlingham, Woldingham, Oxted, Hurst Green Halt, Edenbridge Town, Hever, Cowden, Ashurst, Eridge, Rotherfield, Mayfield, Heathfield, Horam, Hellingly, Hailsham, Polegate, Hampden Park & Heastbourne. Phew!

A terminal station usually gets problems with vagrants and London Bridge was no exception. The more these men and women are moved on, the greater the number that

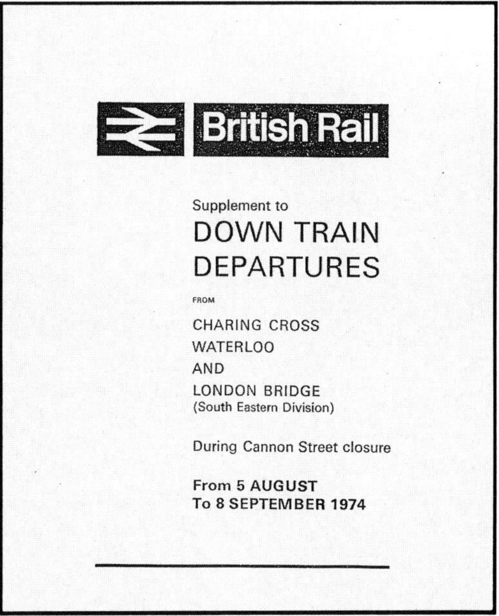
British Rail

Supplement to

DOWN TRAIN DEPARTURES

FROM

CHARING CROSS
WATERLOO
AND
LONDON BRIDGE
(South Eastern Division)

During Cannon Street closure

From 5 AUGUST
To 8 SEPTEMBER 1974

Cannon Street station was closed in the late summer of 1974 to facilitate the laying of new track, and an interim timetable was produced. Some trains were diverted to London Bridge (Central), Charing Cross, Victoria and Blackfriars.

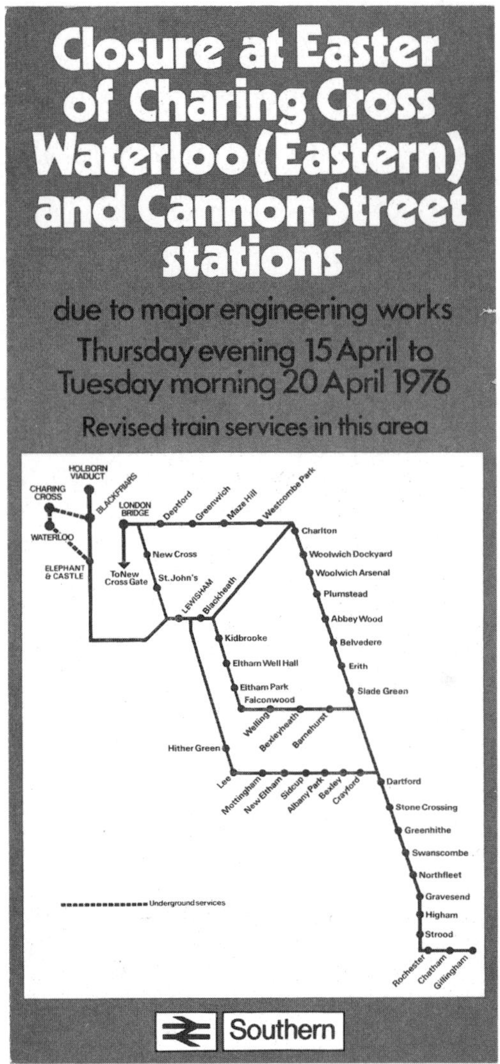

A special timetable was compiled for the Easter 1976 changeover to the new power box at London Bridge.

replaces them. On one occasion, last thing at night, the Supervisor was clearing the station and tried to move a down-and-out without success. In the end the 'tramp' told him to go away as he was a CID officer waiting for a suspect.

Another problem which most stations unfortunately face nowadays is that of vandalism. This is often associated with football crowds, but they are not the only culprits by any means. When a building is getting old it is a ready target for graffiti and damage, but when a pop concert was held at Charlton football ground and we ran special unscheduled trains until well after midnight to bring them back, although there was little public transport to move them home from London Bridge, I am not aware of any damage occurring. Charlton Athletic was, in those days, playing at the Valley, and on a particularly bad Saturday the match was cancelled just as the train was about to leave. I was in a quandary whether to ring the signal box to put the signal back to danger and tell the ticket office that about 400 passengers would be coming back for a ticket refund or make a quick announcement across the platform to the effect that the train would not now run.

On one winter's Saturday when there was a home match at the Valley we suddenly looked up to see the sky full of newspapers and staff running in all directions trying to catch them - some fans had cut the strings of the bundles of evening papers which were on the platforms waiting to be loaded, and being a windy day the catchers' task proved rather hopeless!

About this time we were constantly being worried by 'bomb alerts', false alarms fortunately, although a bomb did explode in a empty coach outside Cannon Street one morning just after the morning peak hour was over. All these warnings meant the stations concerned had to be closed and searched and trains halted. Thus trains were often delayed through no fault whatever of ours.

We had a messenger who took telex messages round the station and was always prepared to fetch us sandwiches or supplies as we could not leave our place of work. If we needed any stationery or stores he would fetch them for us from the Area Office or wherever they came from. Nothing was too much trouble for him and on one particular Saturday afternoon I asked him to fetch me something, forgetting that almost everywhere around London Bridge closes at midday on Saturdays. He eventually reappeared hours later when I was getting very worried about him. Apparently he had searched for a long time to try and get what I wanted, then

In connection with the London Bridge resignalling, a reversible line was put in from the fast lines to the Holborn line a few yards beyond Lewisham. This photograph shows the new layout after the fast line platforms at St Johns had been removed. ***BR***

decided to get on the train and go to Charing Cross to try there. On arrival a bomb alert had been announced and a policeman grabbed him to help search the station, so, not wishing to say that he did not work there, was delayed as a result.

It was not unusual to have to make announcements for 'lost' passengers. On one occasion when we did this, two ladies were reunited but remonstrated with each other, one saying 'You told me to meet you on platform 4A but there isn't one', to which the other replied 'No, I said meet me in the foyer'. I must admit that I never heard any part of a station referred to as a foyer!

It is said that truth is stranger than fiction. Some of the things that happen defy all understanding. During a spell of bad weather when trains were few and far between and very full, a passenger was seen riding on the buffers between the coaches. Perhaps he though he was out in the East!

On another occasion, during warmer weather I might add, a passenger came off a train completely nude, having neatly folded his clothes and handed them in at his local station. It must have been some sort of publicity stunt, as his picture appeared in most newspapers the next day.

One evening, in the rush hour, our attention was drawn to workmen working too close to the track without a look-out, only to find that an old building was being demolished and they were carrying their rubble over electrified lines to a rubbish skip on the other side. They were told of the error of their ways in no uncertain terms!

One day a message was received concerning a dog loose in a compartment. We called the Transport Police, who rode from London Bridge to Charing Cross in an effort to catch it. It transpired that its owner wished to dispose of it, so had put it in the train, shut the door and sent it off.

There was a long strike of refuse collectors in London at about this time and some passengers would bring their refuse on the train and leave it on the station. A member of staff was on duty one morning and saw a passenger leave a parcel behind on the seat. He ran after him with it, pointing out that it must be his. The traveller agreed that it was, but accidentally dropped it only to reveal egg shells, potato peelings, etc, etc.

Of course, when friends knew that I worked in the Control point I had the usual jokes about 'Are you the one who thinks up the excuses?'. I often wonder whether we overdo the business of explanations as the average passenger is not really interested in what has happened and cannot see the connection between his train being late and the incident in question. I heard a railman tell a passenger how late his train would be one day to which the passenger replied 'Thank you for nothing'. I wonder whether that porter will bother to tell the passenger if his train is again delayed. We certainly would not give an untrue explanation, but sometimes the reason for a delay may be due to a suicide or accident to a passenger, and this can bring an invasion of morbid sightseers. It is difficult to write on a board in a few words an explanation of what has taken place, and as a result somewhat hackneyed excuses are put forward.

There was a recent case of a tunnel near Strood being flooded for several weeks due to water seeping through the chalk after a canal had been filled in many years before. As a result the electric current was switched off for safety and diesel trains had to be used for a period. Unfortunately there had been no appreciable rain for a week or two, so the explanation of flooding brought hoots of laughter, and until a special poster was prepared, giving the history of the problem, it meant little. Various remedies were tried and eventually the problem was solved with pumps and by drilling boreholes.

With rail travel, whatever happens either to the track or to a train, the trains behind have to wait or be diverted, sometimes a long way round, and this is something the signalman or 'Control' has to decide. It is rather like a motorway with few exits. If the road is blocked police turn traffic back, but they may gain time by waiting until the road is open again and allowing traffic to continue on its usual way. Here the comparison ceases, as each train has to run in a 'pathway' timing in a given direction, which means that if it is early, late or diverted it is encroaching on another's 'pathway' and delaying that train. In addition, continual signal checks will occur to keep the trains the correct distance apart.

When there is a points or signal failure, a member of staff has to go to the location concerned, possibly on foot or by road, so there is a delay before anything can start. Some stations are unstaffed and some junctions are quite inaccessible by road. If emergency services are required it may mean bringing them over fields to reach the point. When an incident occurs which blocks the lines for a long period of time, trains may have to be terminated short of the obstruction and then the service, stock working and crew's rosters have to be rewritten as a result.

Many of our problems are not of our making, but we suffer as a result, being blamed and put to a lot of expense. For example, an accident to a passenger, a fire, a gas leak, a power failure or a burst water main all mean that trains have to stop, and it is not always possible to predict how long the delay will be. A practice which, unfortunately, is on the increase is that of passengers alighting on the track when a train is delayed. Not only is this dangerous but it also delays everyone longer by the current having to be discharged for passengers' safety, thus stopping all the other trains.

From time to time trains are delayed as passengers are taken ill and perhaps an ambulance has to be called; it is often best to delay the train so that the passenger can remain still until the ambulance arrives. If a passenger falls between the train and platform perhaps the police and fire service have to be summoned, as to move the train could prove fatal. An incident occurred at a station where I worked concerning a passenger who threw his case on to the rack and, in doing so, hit the light tube on the ceiling. A glass splinter fell away and embedded itself in his wrist and it was only because of the quick action of the staff that the passenger did not lose a lot of blood.

Weekend 'possessions' are frequently taken for engineering works with replacement bus services, but from time to time it may be when a motorway is being put over or under the railway. In no way am I trying to give the impression that BR is not to blame for some of its own problems, which may sometimes come about through lack of maintenance or staff problems, but let me give a fictitious example of how a delay snowballs and how the original reason for the delay becomes rather irrelevant.

Let us suppose that the current is switched off outside the carriage sheds in the early morning due to vandalism or a power failure, with the result that empty stock cannot be brought out. Eventually the matter is rectified, and an empty train arrives at Charing Cross to make up a down service. At the station platform alterations have to be made because of its late arrival and, by the time it is ready to leave, a slow train has preceded it. Each time that it reaches a junction the signalman has to decide whether to delay it further to allow another train to cross its path, or give the already late service its head and cause delay to an up train. Connections may have to be abandoned at places such as Tonbridge and Paddock Wood as late departure of those connecting trains would cause delay at Strood, Hastings and Redhill. At Ashford a late arrival would also take the delay to Hastings, and as that line is single a train in the opposite direction would be held up, so both up and down services via Rye would then be late. Our train may now be arriving at Ramsgate late and will make the next service out late, with subsequent delays similar to those above. Possibly these delays could be minimised by cutting short station time, making up time on the journey or by terminating the train short of its destination, but whatever course is adopted passengers will be inconvenienced and complaints will come in which cannot be answered just by saying 'Loss of current outside sidings at....'

Similarly, 'Animals on the line' announced at Cannon Street as the cause of a train being late may bring about hoots of laughter, but passengers in the train when it passed the Weald of Kent may have witnessed it. Some messages are meant purely to warn passengers in advance that delays may be experienced if travelling, for example, via Reading, so passengers may then make alternative arrangements. Maybe our notices are too brief and give the wrong impression and alternatives are not suggested.

Strangely enough, rail passengers will be heard to say 'The train kept stopping and starting - I don't know why', but if in a car or coach the explanation from the passenger would be different: 'The roads were packed. I felt sorry for the poor driver. First of all the road was up, then the traffic lights were out of order and, to crown it all, cows were wandering about in the road.'

Staff shortages are often blamed for trains not running; naturally, spare men must be kept to an absolute minimum, so if a man starting work at perhaps 4 am is delayed because his motor cycle or car is faulty, his train cannot run. Bad weather always brings its share of complaints. One can have 99 sets of points out of 100 working perfectly, but one out of order is enough to delay all services at that point. Enormous amounts of money are spent each year in combating snow and ice when possibly there may be only two major freeze-ups per winter. I expect quite a few passengers would admit to taking longer in getting to the station in their car or on foot in adverse weather conditions if they were honest. One cannot stop rain or snow falling, but measures are made to minimise the inconvenience. As most of our rolling-stock is 'garaged' out of doors, icing up is made easier!

More and more devices have been introduced for information to passengers in the form of 'long line announcements' by signalmen, VDU screens and telex machines, but they are only as good as the men operating them. The media delight in knocking BR, but an old porter once told me that he remembered that in the 1920s the service got so bad that questions were raised 'in the House' about his line. I once asked a well-known radio personality who used my station whether he really hated BR, as he gave that impression over the air, but he said no, and likened it to the jokes he made about his wife! I agree that certain areas get more than their share of troubles. Perhaps the Tonbridge-Hastings line is a case in point as, over the years, some locos and coaches have been disallowed over that line because of gauge restriction and long-term engineering work, but let us hope that those days are over. Similarly, passengers from East Croydon say that when things are bad at Charing Cross their service is the first to terminate at London Bridge. This is true, because the stock and crews always work straight 'in and out', so do not affect other services if taken out.

I cannot help thinking that at times BR is too sensitive about its short-comings and invites comments by telling passengers to whom to write and saying, for example, 'The staff here have been on a customer care course', which invites a reply! Or 'No more queues with our new ticket issuing machines'!

During my first seven years at London Bridge I saw many changes and several things accomplished that had been talked about for years, so felt that it was time for a change. I was successful in being appointed to a post which was connected with the timetable at London Bridge signal box in computer form (it had never been my intention to seek unusual jobs on BR but I have certainly been in some!). This job involved feeding timetable information into a computer, with its subsequent weekly and daily alterations, to operate the indicators at Waterloo East and London Bridge (SE) automatically. The idea was that Dartford, Feltham and, later, Victoria signal boxes' data would also go in for the same purpose. The computer would also print out a full day's punctuality details by comparing the timetable with actual performance, listing each train by its number at each reporting point - any glaring errors in our work could be seen on the print-out. The computer would enter each train up to 1 hour before or 1 hour after its booked time. This time limit was set for two reasons; one was that a train number would be used more than once a day as otherwise there would not be enough to go round, and second empty and freight trains often run quite a few minutes before time. The print-out for a certain passenger train may look like this:

2L12 CX + 01 LB + 02 LM + 04 WA + 03

meaning 1 minute late from Charing Cross, 2 minutes late at London Bridge, 4 minutes adrift at Lewisham and 3 minutes behind time at Woolwich Arsenal.

Punched tape and computers were a new field to me and it took me a while to understand what it was all about. At that time it was still in its infancy; more than once our computer 'went down' and all our information had to be reloaded. With the system in question, automatic route setting on the signal box panel and automatic insertion of train numbers would have been a possibility, but with the constant changeovers of rolling-stock and replatforming at terminal stations, at that time it was shelved.

Ticket office work still interested me, so sooner or later I thought I would return to it. There were always ticket office vacancies on BR but for much of the time no recruiting took place, so, with early retirements, there were numerous posts to fill either with overtime (in the London area, anyway), by taking on new staff, or not covering some of the hours at all. I have often thought that part-time station staff could be used for the peaks, or perhaps at the time of a fare increase, maybe even recalling retired men in some cases for perhaps 15 hours per week.

Eventually I found myself back in a ticket office again, but things had changed and it was necessary for me to have a brief 'refresher'. It would appear that as fares are increased (usually annually), at the same time new cheap facilities are being introduced, mainly for off-peak travel, which makes the fares structure very confusing to staff and passengers alike. No doubt many of BR's complaints about wrong fares being charged are as a result of this.

* * *

There are, of course, many railway enthusiasts who do not work for BR and look on the railway as a hobby without all the day-to-day problems and 'aggro' which go with it. Things have, understandably, changed since I joined BR, some for the better, for example working conditions and hours, and leave entitlements (for a number of years we only got a day 'in lieu' for working some Bank Holidays and extra pay for some, but later this was made uniform and all public holidays now earn an extra day's holiday if they are worked, as well as extra pay). There was a service on Christmas Day and Boxing Day until the 1960s, then it gradually thinned out, certain stations were closed, fewer trains ran each year, and first Christmas Day and then Boxing Day lost their service.

Electrification has been extended and new lines opened, such as Thameslink, but we are still inclined to think that everything since Beeching is negative. The work today is very different with modern computers, but one can be excused for looking back on the 'good old days' when stations were liberally staffed, vandalism was almost unknown, and each station had its own signal box, shunting yard, and station master, and there was the Divisional Office of which one lived in awe.

I hope I have given you some insight into my life on the railway. As with other jobs, some days had their lighter moments whilst others were very trying, but on balance I think I have seen a side of life which, had I not been born on, lived on and worked on the railway, I would not have experienced. So may I leave you with a few anecdotes accumulated over the years 'from the other side of the window'.

Epilogue
TICKET OFFICE TALES
...or 'a man for all seasons'

Working as a booking clerk in the London area is definitely more demanding than in a non-London area station, as tickets to the London area are kept and accounted for separately. London area and certain perimeter stations do not carry a three-month validity for ordinary return tickets and different validities apply to off-peak tickets. In addition, the arrangement for season tickets issued to the Underground has changed several times. When I first went into a ticket office a separate season ticket was issued to each Underground station. These were then brought into zones, which changed from time to time until eventually the zones included BR stations and buses. Some rates went down considerably and, as a result of the first change, refunds were given to passengers until it was ruled that the fares system was illegal and it was modified. Passengers also changed over from a BR-only season to a Capitalcard, as they were eventually called. The clerk at a London terminal station unquestionably has slightly the easier task, apart from the volume of passengers, as there is usually a separate window for season tickets and enquiries, and all fare books and timetables are based on London. At a suburban station possibly the clerk works alone and there is no one to give him a meal break and, at the time of a fares increase, he has to amend all his documents himself.

I also have a great deal of sympathy for platform and barrier staff, particularly late at night when alone. Life can be very unpleasant if any trouble is experienced - if a passenger objects to you asking for a ticket or doesn't like the colour of your skin - since usually help is a long way away. Attacks on staff occur all too frequently and I wonder that we ever get staff in some areas, and understand, up to a point, that they adopt the attitudes they do.

*　　*　　*

When I returned to ticket office work, railcards had recently been introduced for the young, the old and families, and I was amused to see on a passenger's application form under 'hobbies' that a poor old soul of 80 was interested in shark fishing and mountaineering. I expect she had her tongue in her cheek, but the next was more optimistic, 'looking for a rich husband'. In recent years each season ticket holder has come to require a photocard, and a child needs something to show that he/she is under 16 years of age, so to issue one some proof of date of birth is required. When a child was asked for this verification recently, she replied 'I know my date of birth'. I suppose she thought it was a memory jogger for herself!

*　　*　　*

Passengers never expect to wait more than a few minutes at a ticket office window whereas they will queue quite quietly at the corner shop or village post office without banging on the ledge or shouting 'When am I going to be served?' I have seen passengers queue for a minute or two and, when it is their turn, delay others through not having found their railcard or money. Also, it is strange that if a train is due immediately the passenger is very grateful, but if the next is not scheduled for 30 minutes the clerk often gets the blame for it! Other passengers frequently complain of cyclists who bring their bikes into the queue instead of parking them a few feet away. One day I actually saw a cyclist take his cycle into a tea queue at a London terminal station and then get in everyone's way as he had not got sufficient hands for tea, bike and rolls.

Some towns have their local civic society which tends to take an active part in current affairs. At a place where I once worked the local society arranged to have the front of the station repainted, but also stopped announcements being made after the morning peak period as it disturbed the residents; they also insisted that a redundant gateway be replaced as Queen Victoria had once used it, asked for detonators to be exploded more quietly, came out in the night to stop sand blasting being carried out, and requested that freight trains should not run through at night!

I have already mentioned the vagrants, etc, who are to be found at large stations, but in addition elderly people and youths (not necessarily 'gricers') spend many hours there probably for the sake of the company of other people. Some old men turn up at the station at about 7 am and are to be seen on and off most of the day. At one station where I worked the same elderly woman brought sweets in most days and would ask for each clerk by name, one by one, usually asking for the ones she couldn't see until eventually she would say 'You had better have these' and hand over the sweets. Others would come along in a very doddery state and ask for a very difficult journey - usually the same one each time - knowing that they could never undertake it. Yet another woman would come to the station and say 'I'm lost' and give a telephone number to ring. Until we knew her we rang the number in question only to find that she had left there about 20 years before and was now in a local old people's home.

A few years ago certain village booking offices were also the local post office - for example Sole Street and Amberley - so it was not uncommon for a passenger to ask for a ticket to London with their pension and six first class stamps! The two lots of money had to be kept separate, and usually more parcels were sent by post than rail from those stations. The work was normally undertaken by the signalman, so the post had to be advertised (on the internal vacancy list) as 'knowledge of ticket and post office work'. Rather difficult to acquire! At one of these post offices cum railway stations, the telephone was on a party line with the call box outside, and was of the type where the caller would lift the receiver and wait for the operator to ask what number was required. The calls from the station had to be prefixed with the words 'Sub postmaster's call' so that the call was not charged. It struck me that if users of the call box outside knew of this arrangement they could get a free call, as presumably the operator could not tell where the call originated.

One of the main problems of going somewhere to which you are not accustomed is getting to know the routine and where things are kept. On 'late turn' one can ask the person who is going off, but on opening up one has to do it the hard way! When I was doing some temporary relief work a few years earlier I went to a station 'early turn' one Sunday and found the station in a state of rebuilding. Although there was a temporary office, the safe was in the remains of the old office.

I found the safe and had been given all the keys, but no one had told me that the bag in the front of the safe was an 'alarm' bag and would make a terrific noise when moved. I expect it woke the entire town, but no one came to see what was wrong. At another office which was being altered the safe was in a tiny room and it was necessary for me to go in there on completion of my turn. I put the key in the keyhole, turned it and went in; the door slammed behind me with my key outside. It was very dark and there was no keyhole on the inside, so I had to climb up a little ledge, look out of the fanlight over the door and peer through a space about 2 inches wide. I called out to anyone I saw and asked to be let out, but about the first six passengers walked away, no doubt thinking it was *Candid Camera*.

I remember going to a station one evening for a few hours and, as usual, the clerk was getting ready to go. He showed me what was required and left the office, leaving an attractive young lady with me. I had presumed that she had come to escort him home, but now I was in a bit of a quandary - if the station manager had come along and seen her I doubt whether he would have accepted the excuse that 'I found her there'. After a while it transpired that she was a policewoman waiting for someone.

A number of us did overtime at other stations from time to time as there were almost always vacancies somewhere and, if your station was up to establishment, others would often ring up for help. I will call the man in my next story 'Bill'. He was one of those who worked in an outer suburban office and did overtime in the evening peak period at one of the London terminal stations. As one might expect, the same passengers appeared at London in the evenings as went up in the mornings and one said 'Did I not see you at my station this morning?' Bill said 'That was my brother - give him a message for me.' And so the messages went to and fro from Bill to Bill via the passenger. He was rather grateful to be sent somewhere else before the matter got out of hand. I don't know if the man ever suspected he was being conned.

It is not always the passengers who are conned - I was on a number of occasions. Perhaps confused is a better description, as I did not know whether the couple in question were intentionally 'sending me up' or not. I have tried various ways over the years of asking travellers what type of ticket they want, but each way lends itself to misunderstanding. I asked this passenger 'Are you coming back today?' The lady said 'No', so I sold her a Day Return. 'But,' she said, 'I'm not going today.' Determined not to fall into the same trap again, I asked the next person 'Are you coming back the same day?' His answer was 'Yes, the same day as she is'.

It is not uncommon for a passenger to ask for a ticket 'on tick'. This, of course, is not done, but we knew some of our regulars so well that we would put the money in the till and get them to repay us later, but a passenger asked me to do this one day and, when I explained that I would loan her the money, she said 'In that case give me a return and an Underground ticket as well'. Yet another passenger wanted a ticket but was not known to me and had nothing valuable to leave except a spanner. I felt very guilty as I suppose I should have given nuts and bolts as change. (Perhaps it wasn't his spanner anyway.)

If a passenger is genuinely without funds and a relative pays the fare at another station (plus a small fee), a ticket can be issued to the stranded passenger. It is at times difficult to make the passenger understand that he must make the arrangements first by telephone for his friends to come to the station and pay. It would not be practical to keep him prisoner pending payment!

It is easy to misunderstand exactly which station a passenger wishes to travel to, such as Ashford or Rainham where there are more than one, and no doubt passengers have gone to the wrong one over the years, but it was about 5 pm when a young man and his girl came along and asked for two Day Returns to Sandown. I questioned whether they could get there and back the same evening but they assured me that they could. Without a murmur they paid up but came back a few days later complaining bitterly that they wanted Sandown Park at Esher. Margate can get mistaken for Moorgate, but it took us some time to realise that some daily foreign passengers wished to go to Whitechapel and not Whitstable!

Some passengers ask the fare and the time of the next train every time they travel although they go at the same time every day, whilst others will have the correct change on every occasion. We only get to know a few passengers' names and hence describe them to the other clerks as 'The New Cross man who always has the right money', or 'the Hayes lady who always has the £20 note'. It is an old music hall joke to say 'A return please', 'Where to?', 'Back here of course', but a few passengers do that every day; or they ask for the station name where they already are. Some ask for newspapers or cigarettes in error; I suppose they rehearse what they are going to buy that morning and go to the wrong place first. Believe it or not, we had a lady at the window one morning who just wouldn't believe that it was not the post office. As the office was glass-fronted and nothing could seen but tickets and seasons, I could not understand her mistake.

Our passengers sometimes find it difficult to know which ticket window to use and when one asked the clerk if he sold season tickets he said 'Yes, I am a man for all seasons'! Similarly, when a passenger left his change behind, someone behind was heard to say 'That's the problem with the young generation - won't accept change'!

From time to time members of the public ask if a poster can be exhibited for a fete, etc. But the one that I thought took the biscuit was a letter from a lad asking us to exhibit a poster looking for a girl whom he wanted to get to know after having seen her a month before on the station.

When we know our passengers a humorous reply sometimes goes down well - in fact, some people expect it. The usual answer to 'Higham single' is 'I wish I was'; or to 'How do I get to Oxford?' could be 'There are a lot of exams to pass first'. Our customers are quite delighted if we know their destination before they ask, but if they wish to change it they have to get in very quickly.

After a while the clerk becomes accustomed to nicknames for tickets - the Capitalcard is often called the 'capitalist card', the runabout ticket a 'runaway ticket', or a ticket for the Underworld instead of the Underground, and so on. There are also sometimes requests for 'confession' (concession) tickets, but I must confess to having been totally baffled by a request for 'Chinese clothes'. After repeating this a few times in an Asian dialect I realised that it must be Charing Cross (try it yourself and see).

Another story concerns the passenger who did not mind what ticket he had so long as it did not have the originating station name on it. I can only assume that he didn't ought to have been where he was, and possibly wished to claim for expenses from somewhere else.

A rather upset young man called in one afternoon explaining how the train had gone away with his luggage in it. We sympathised and asked him how it had happened. He said 'I put my bags in the train and went up the steps and across the road to buy a can of drink, and when I got back the train was gone.' (Imagine this - it was a suburban intermediate station where each train stops about 30 seconds.)

I was working at a London terminal station one morning when things went wrong and the station had to be closed as there were no trains. The doors were closed as a safety measure and hundreds of passengers accumulated outside. The enquiry and ticket office staff bear the full brunt of the public's criticism when things are bad, and on that day one of the clerks had gone out in his railway jacket to try and buy some food, only to find on his return that the station was locked. The last we saw of him, he had an armful of fish and chips, was surrounded by angry passengers banging on the door, and was saying 'Let me in'!

Having been brought up in the country, I was always very aware in the difference in the pace of life in the London area. This was particularly noticeable in my next story, which took place on my journey home on a suburban electric train. The train was formed of corridor coaching stock, which was unusual, and I could tell that my fellow travellers were strangers. The train stopped at their station and one said to the other 'I thinks us be yer', whereupon she slowly took the cases down from the rack and slid back the corridor door. At this juncture the train restarted, but the good lady was not too concerned. She said simply 'They dawn't givee long yer, do em?', closed the door and put all the belongings back on the rack. Of course, at the next stop exactly the same thing happened. At the third stop they managed to alight, but without a word of complaint or surprise. They just got off and, I presume, waited for a train back.

A major innovation was the APTIS machine for ticket issues. This has done away with conventional tickets and, instead, larger thinner cards are loaded into the machine's hopper and printed as a customer requires. In addition, season tickets and seat reservations are dealt with in this way and a cash balance, quickly made from a figure provided by the machine, has minimised the clerk's work substantially.

All tickets were now very thin, and some 'customers' (as they are now called) did not at first recognise season tickets and railcards for what they were. In fact, frequently passengers were seen to write the times or stations to change on the tickets, thinking that they were purely till receipts. They thought that we were being unreasonable if we remonstrated with them and pointed out that an Inspector would think that they had been defacing their ticket. We had always had a large number of seasons lost, but these increased alarmingly when APTIS first came in, for that reason.

Some of the schoolchildren were the worst offenders for losing their seasons, the same ones each term. I think that the 'strong arm' bullies took the other pupils' tickets, but this, of course, was made more difficult when photocards were required.

When a traveller reported a season as lost, we would take all necessary details and suggest that he or she enquired again after a few days, as some were returned by post or from another station. When one such season ticket holder asked if his ticket had turned up, I asked 'When did you lose it?' 'About a year ago,' he replied. I ventured to suggest that perhaps he had left the matter rather too long.

I often sit through a comedy programme unmoved, but when I see a funny incident in real life I cannot contain my laughter. One such instance was, again, on my homeward journey one night. Some waiting passengers hang about round the ticket barrier, a practice that would annoy me if I was the collector. On this occasion, one of the group was the 'stock broker' type with bowler, rolled umbrella and pin-striped suit. A labourer, covered in cement and dirt and in his working gear, handed his ticket to the city gent, realised his mistake and said 'Sorry, guv, I thought you were the **** ticket bloke.'

INDEX